PLANT AGRICULTURE

PLANT AGRICULTURE

Federal Biotechnology
Activities

by

Carolyn Bloch

np NOYES PUBLICATIONS
Park Ridge, New Jersey, U.S.A.

Published in the United States of America by
Noyes Publications
Mill Road, Park Ridge, New Jersey 07656

10 9 8 7 6 5 4 3 2 1

Library of Congress Cataloging-in-Publication Data

Bloch, Carolyn.
    Plant agriculture.

    Includes index.
    1. Crops--Research--United States. 2. Agriculture--
Research--United States. 3. Biotechnology--Research--
United States. 4. Crops--Research--Government policy--
United States. 5. Agriculture--Research--Government
policy--United States. 6. Biotechnology--Research--
Government policy--United States. I. Title.
SB52.U6B53 1986   631'.072'073   85-24665
ISBN 0-8155-1058-6

Foreword

This book presents an overview along with in-depth information on the principal Federal policies, issues, and research in biotechnology that pertain specifically to plant agriculture. The U.S. government presently has considerable involvement and funding in biotechnology research, and is continuing to emphasize the need for this research in the agencies already involved in agricultural research along with the agencies that have agricultural related programs.

This book points out that U.S. government policies and issues must be resolved in a way that government, universities, and industry can work together in order to achieve viable and productive results. Additionally there must continue to be federal research support in this field along with private research in order to enhance our potential for future commercialization. Hopefully this will help the U.S. to find solutions to worldwide food problems, to increase our agricultural trade, and enable the U.S. to continue to assume leadership in the new and exciting biotechnology industry.

Contents

1

Introduction

Even though research in plant genetic engineering is long term and high risk, research in this field will be absolutely essential in order to meet the future food needs of world-wide populations. Therefore, It is very important for all countries with high technology resources to increase crop yields, to improve the quality of crops, and to increase plant resistance to pests and environmental conditions. Breakthroughs in this field could also significantly increase farm efficiency, profitability and this in turn will greatly help the U.S. to maintain a competitive advantage in international agricultural trade.

In order to pursue these technical advances and leadership, the application of many new research techniques in plant agriculture will be needed. Scientists and researchers trained in the basic sciences such as molecular biology, microbiology, physiology, biochemistry and plant pathology will have to enlarge their knowledge and highly skilled training to include an understanding of gene structure, transfer and regulation.

Efforts to understand basic cellular and genetic processes began thousands of years ago when tribes noticed that all seeds from similar plants were not equal in their production vigor. They had no understanding of how this worked but over the centuries this selection process slowly resulted in improved crops.

In the latter part of the 19th century Gregor Mendel performed many breeding experiments. Through continued research, biologists in the 1900's were able to find out valuable information on chromosomes and how this determines various traits. After years of research, scientists were able to work with whole plants and achieve improved varieties through complex crosses and backcrosses. By the 1930's and 1950's hybrid corn plants were introduced and this dramatically increased crop production.

However, there are several disadvantages in this type of process, as it used the entire plant and took repeated backcrosses, and in many cases, it also required generations and years to produce improvements.

Exciting new developments are now taking place in molecular biology and genetic engineering. Molecular biologists are working on a molecular level as compared to the past efforts of plant breeders that only worked on the entire plant, and so the new genetic engineering techniques will combine with the conventional breeding techniques to produce many new changes in the agricultural field.

Over the past 20 years, molecular biology has moved from an exploratory, academic science to a practical technology. The science has advanced from the identification of the genetic material in all cells (deoxyribonucleic acid or DNA) to deciphering the relationship between the order of chemical groups along the DNA molecule and the structure of proteins (the ultimate products of most genes).

A gene is that entity which passed down from parent cell to daughter cell, endows all of the potentially vast number of offspring with the capability to display a specific function. Genes are regions along DNA molecules, and DNA, a threadlike molecule, carries information in a linear array of chemical groups like the paper tape which feeds instructions to a telex machine. Several hundred to several thousand of these groups called bases, make up each gene. The DNA molecule in a single bacterium is about three million bases long, whereas each human cell contains DNA molecules whose total length is about three billion bases.

The usual function of a gene is to produce a protein, a molecule consisting of connected strings of chemical groups called amino acids. Each protein, containing from about thirty to a thousand or more amino acids, folds to form a structure which has one or more specific functions. Certain proteins can carry out chemical reactions (enzymes), while others have the ability to affect responses of organs (hormones). Other types of proteins bind together to form structures such as muscle fiber or the coat of a virus.

Classical genetics has identified many of the genes in bacteria which determine useful chemical reactions. Modern techniques include the ability to alter such genes deliberately to make more of their products and thus create commercially useful micro-organisms. Advances in molecular biology allow scientists to move single or multiple genes from the cells of one organism and to insert them into cells of another species. This last development, coupled with the ability to identify the complete chemical structure of genes and to cut, trim, synthesize, and connect parts of genes to make new combinations, offers the ability of making "to order" both micro-organisms and proteins of commercial value.

Today gene splicing or rDNA technology is the prime high technology focus in agricultural research. The process involves four steps. These steps include identifying, locating and purifying genes, isolating the gene from the others on the chromosome, constructing vectors to deliver the genes, and lastly cloning, duplicating or inserting the gene into the host cell.

This process is very complex and there are many problems that will have to be solved in order to take the gene splicing process and produce viable results. The major roadblocks to creating improved plant varieties on a routine basis is that many more years of research will be needed to understand and work with vectors, perform gene expression, use cell culture methods, and engineer photosynthesis.

Important research is now being conducted that hopefully will help solve some of the mysteries surrounding plant genetics including the study of vectors. Vectors are used to deliver genetic information to plants. Scientists have changed the gene structure in plants by using Ti plasmid (a vector that inserts new DNA into plant cells) found in crown gall tumors which are induced by Agrobacterium tumefaciens.

Researchers working on petunias in culture were able to insert an antibiotic bacterial gene into the DNA portion of a Ti plasmid but while experiments on vectors have taken place on plants infected with Agrobacterium, more work has to be done on plants not infected with Agrobacterium such as corn, rice, and wheat.

Progress has also taken place in plant virus experiments to see if they can be used as possible vectors. The prime consideration and hope with plant viruses is that viruses infect many plants while the Ti plasmid vector is limited to a few plants. Scientists are also studying the use of liposome chloroplast transformations to insert DNA fragments into plant cells. A great deal of work is being done in these research areas and also in studying other types of possible vectors.

Other constraints to genetic engineering that need to be studied concern research on gene expression which involves inserting a foreign gene into a higher organism. Molecular biologists are studying the elements that can control and regulate gene expression. Scientists have identified more than 60,000 expressed genes in higher plants but the actual numbers run into the millions.

While applying the techniques of gene splicing in the laboratories is important, scientists are also studying cell culture methodology in order to grow cells from plants in the laboratories. The technique of cell cultures bridges the gap between molecular genetics and plant breeding. If single plant cells can be cultivated, selected, and regenerated, many millions of cells in cultures can be studied and several species of a plant can be cultured and regenerated at one time. Some progress has been made and it is now possible to culture tobacco, rice, carrots, and potato cells, but many crops won't regenerate from cell cultures such as legumes and grass crop species.

Another research area of great interest is in the study of photosynthesis which is the process by which plants capture light energy and fix carbon dioxide into organic form. Many universities are doing research on some aspects of photosynthesis. Much of this research involves biology, physics and chemistry because studies in all of these fields is necessary to understand photosynthesis. However a great deal of research still needs to be done before scientists will have the working knowledge and be able to engineer photosynthesis to significantly increase the yields of crops.

There are many constraints and difficulties that scientists must master in recombinant DNA as applied to plants.

Research in all of these areas is continuing but the areas of more immediate promise are in the applications of recombinant DNA such as in transferring the traits of plants, the study of bacteria to combat diseases, and in the area of nitrogen fixation. Therefore the applications of rDNA is the primary research thrust of companies involved in plant genetics today.

Some promising research areas also involve transferring the traits of plants which will develop new varieties superior to those on the market. These will produce higher yields and better overall performance as they will have improved disease and insect resistance and also have greater stress tolerance. Presently these breeding techniques along with recombinant DNA are being conducted by several companies in the U.S.

For instance DeKalb-Pfizer Genetics has PH.D's working at stations throughout this country on various breeding programs. The Plant Genetics Research in Groton Connecticut and The Bioscience Department in DeKalb Illinois are jointly involved in developing new breeding techniques to make genetic improvements in such crops as corn and soybeans.

At Pioneer Hi Bred International, research efforts in hybrid performance include corn, hybrid sorghum, alfalfa, wheat, soybeans, and cotton and they are now conducting initial research in the development of hybrid sunflowers. Other companies that see promising results in this field include American Cyanamid who is now collaborating with Molecular Genetics Inc. to develop superior lines and varieties of corn and other cereals.

Martin Marietta is also involved in joint ventures with Chiron Corporation of San Francisco and NPI of Salt Lake City to develop commodity crops with superior yields and increased resistance to pests and diseases. Monsanto working in this field has transferred the active agent of a biological control to a strain of bacteria on corn roots, and plans to field test this genetically engineered pesticide.

Scientists have been very successful in working on the external properties of plants and particularly important results have been produced in working on plant bacteria. One of the most promising areas in this research has been in frost protection bacteria. Scientists have been successful in finding viruses that kill bacteria. It was found that there was a correlation between the bacteria of the plant and the temperature at which the plant is damaged by frost. If the bacteria is removed, ice on the plants will form at lower temperatures and can save many plants from frost damage.

Research in this area has been going on at the University of California and the University of Colorado. Advanced Genetic Sciences is working with the University of California on this research and working on the use of naturally occurring and chemically mutated ice strains. Frost Technology Corporation is also doing extensive research in this field and is using technology originally invented at the University of Colorado. In protecting plants from frost, however, they are not using a genetically engineered product, because they are using bioactive agents to kill the surface ice nucleating bacteria on plants.

Biological nitrogen fixation, another promising research program, includes extending nitrogen fixing bacterial systems to a wider variety of plants, transferring the bacterial nitrogen fixing genes to plants and making existing nitrogen fixing systems more efficient. Studies in this field will help scientists to understand how nitrogen fixing genes are regulated and how they respond to environmental levels of nitrogen and oxygen. Companies such as Agrigenetics and Biotechnica are actively involved in researching nitrogen fixation.

One aspect in studying nitrogen fixation involves studying soil bacteria. Advanced Genetic Sciences is doing research on Rhizobium. This bacteria nodulates plant roots and makes it possible for soybeans and other legumes to fix their own nitrogen from the atmosphere thereby reducing the need for fertilizers. The company is investigating new ways to genetically engineer and improve rhizobium strains.

At the present time even with all of the research being done in government laboratories, universities, and private industry, it may be 10 years or more before crop production will be effected by these research efforts. If the U.S can provide larger expenditures for basic and applied sciences so that scientists can do long term research and in turn help universities and private industry, if the policy and regulatory issues can be settled for the benefit of all, then undoubtably there will be great advances in biotechnology in the U.S. and in other countries with high technology resources.

Part I

Federal Policies and Issues

2

Federal Support for Plant Agriculture Biotechnology Research

In order for the U.S. to be a leader in biotechnology, many knowledgable individuals in the field feel that the Federal government needs a long term commitment to basic and applied research in biotechnology. The purpose of public sector research is to provide basic new knowledge, techniques and expertise which in turn will be available to industry. Basically industry funding itself is based upon the existence of a stable university research community and this in turn depends on a substantial level of support from the federal government.

Public and private research organizations have fundamentally different research roles within the broad spectrum of basic, applied, and developmental research. For example, basic research accounted for about 40% of all food and agricultural research funded by USDA and the states in FY 83. The Agricultural Research Service (ARS) devoted 49 percent of its funds to mission oriented basic research in FY 83 while only 10% of industry research in the food and agricultural sciences is devoted to basic research.

In the past agricultural research traditionally has been performed at land grant universities which are supported by federal and state funds. In the past these universities have made important contributions and innovations in agriculture, but these land grant universities have not been in the forefront of new technologies because until recently they used their research funding to meet the immediate needs of the farmer.

However, today this existing agricultural research system in the land grant university setting provides an advantageous situation for applying advances in biotechnology to agriculture. The system can supply scientific expertise in science as well as interrelated programs of applied research, and technology transfer capabilities.

Federal expenditures in FY 1983 totaled $200 million dollars for plant biology research at doctorate granting institutions. The Federal government provided about one-half of the support, and the state governments provided one-third with the balance coming from the private sector. Essentially plant biology research and training is concentrated in land grant institutions. They received 83% of the total research support and employed 80% of the faculty in this field.

Primarily Federal funding for the agricultural research

system is through USDA which today funds research and education programs of $1,242 million in support of agriculture and forestry. However, other agencies are also involved in agricultural research and have received substantial funding for their projects.

Basically USDA's agricultural in-house research funding is through their Agricultural Research Service (ARS) with a total budget of over $487 million in FY 1985 while their plant and animal biotechnology research funding is $15.4 million with research being conducted on 114 biotechnology projects.

The Cooperative State Research Service (CSRS) is another arm of USDA that is involved in agricultural research and funded approximately 46 million dollars in FY 85. CSRS has funded or is currently funding biotechnology research to the states through the following legislative acts enacted by Congress.

The Hatch Experiment Station Act-provides for at least one experiment station in each state to conduct research basic to the problems of agriculture in its broadest sense. The act supports research for agriculture, forestry, and rural life and these funds are the largest of those that CSRS administers.

The McIntire-Stennis Cooperative Forestry Research Act-supports forestry research at 60 institutions. The act provides for forestry research and the development of a trained pool of forestry scientists and mangagers.

Public Law 95-113-Section 1445 -provides research funding through CSRS for the 16 land grant colleges of 1890 and

Tuskegee Institute. Research directors administer agricultural research at black land-grant institutions.

Public Law 95-113 Section 1433 & 1434-provides Federal funding to State agricultural experiment stations and 28 eligible schools and colleges of veterinary medicine for their research in animal health and disease.

Public Law 89-106-Under this law CSRS administers the special grants programs for basic and applied research at nonprofit institutions of higher education or nonprofit organizations. Funds are provided for high priority regional or national research in such areas as genetic improvement of crops, development of integrated pest management systems, improvement of semiarid rangelands and increase understanding of human nutrient requirements. In FY 1985, the special grants program was funded at $3.4 million, however, the special grants program has been eliminated.

Public Law 89-106 -Under this law CSRS administers the competitive grants program. Under this competitive grants program, research is now being conducted in photosynthesis, biological nitrogen fixation, genetic mechanisms for crop improvement, human nutrition, and biological stress of plants.

The biotechnology initiative within the Competitive Grants Program has received support from the National Association of State Universities and Land Grant Colleges, the President's Advisor, the Board on Agriculture of the National Academy of

Sciences, the National Science Foundation and biotechnology companies.

The CSRS plant sciences and animals grant program previously had $9.5 million available for grants in these fields. If you combine this amount with the new biotechnology initiative in the competitive grants program there is now approximately a total of $29.5 million in grants to be awarded to biotechnology projects in FY 85.

It was decided to put the biotechnology initiative in the Competitive Grants Program because this program attracts scientists with appropriate training in biotechnology. Data indicates that about one-quarter of competitive grant funds are directly used to hire graduate and post graduate students to assist in the research. Secondly, the scope of institutions or organizations eligible to compete for grants under this program is broader than the Special Grants program. In 1983, there were 16 grants awarded to private nonprofit organizations. Private industry is permitted to participate in these grants but because of the fact that all the information resulting from this research is public, private industry generally does not participate.

The USDA Forest Service also has a small research program that is involved in genetic engineering with a budget for FY 85 of approximately $2 million dollars, however, it is anticipated that there will be budget cuts in the future.

Additionally other Federal agencies, industry, and State

sources provide significant funding for research and education programs related to agriculture and forestry, and in FY 1983, they spent an estimated $3.7 billion, about three times the level of USDA funding for that year. In FY 1981, other federal agencies other than USDA spent $629.5 million on Federal food and agricultural research programs.

FY 1981* -Dollars in Millions

Agency For International Development	108.7
Department of Commerce	72.5
Department of Defense	25.0
Department of Energy	36.5
Environmental Protection Agency	13.5
Health & Human Services	193.8
Department of Interior	103.9
International Trade Commission	1.4
Department Of Labor	2.6
NASA	25.0
National Science Foundation	24.5
TVA	19.5
Veterans Administration	2.6
TOTAL	$629.5

*Funding levels for FY 84 & 85 for agencies involved in agricultural research other than USDA are not compiled each year.

All of these agencies support programs that relate to agriculture. For instance agencies such as NSF support research in universities and other institutions in the basic biological and physical sciences, NASA supports research in remote sensing, the Department of Energy supports research in energy production, the Agency for International Development supports agricultural research in developing countries, the Department of Defense develops new food items to meet military needs, and Health and Human Services (NIH & FDA) is involved in biomedical research and in the regulatory issues that pertain to the field of biotechnology.

With all of the funding in agricultural research, Federal support for plant molecular biology, tissue culture and basic physiology development and metabolism has not increased in the past few years. However, some additional Federal assistance has been provided to new small firms and this includes many new biotechnology firms.

For instance the Small Business Innovation Development Act passed in 1982 created SBIRs. This was enacted to increase the share of Federal R&D monies going to small businesses by directing that small firms receive at least a fixed minimum percentage of R&D awards made by Federal agencies with sizable R&D development budgets. U.S. funding of applied research in biotechnology is provided principally through this act. USDA presently has 6 research areas that include forest and related resources, plant production and protection, animal production and protection, air, water and soils, food and human nutrition, and rural and community development.

In response to the June 1983 deadline, USDA received 274 proposals from small businesses that had innovative approaches to solve problems in U.S. agriculture. This act gives the Federal government an opportunity to help small biotechnology firms in plant agriculture.

During the next several years, the Federal government is expected to focus on indirect means of encouraging private industry to increase its long term research investments and on improving the climate for commercializing the results of its R&D activities. The Federal government has provided assistance to R&D firms through the Economy Recovery Act of 1981 which includes R&D tax credits, acceleration depreciation schedules, and other incentives to slim R&D investments. The legislation was enacted to try to help R&D firms with tax credits that in turn would increase R&D spending in private industry in this country. However the tax credits are not as helpful to new biotechnology firms for several reasons.

New biotechnology firms use limited partnerships as an important source of financing and the most favorable tax treatment of income for R&D limited partnerships is in the IRS code Section 1235 .This applies to all substantial rights to a patent by any holder and under this code any royalties received as a result of transfer of a patent qualify as long-term capital gains rather than ordinary income. Presently under the Plant Variety Protection Act plant variety protection certificates are exempt, and many companies feel that the tax code should apply to these certificates.

Secondly new biotechnology firms are faced with financial constraints that could be helped if the current depreciation schedule which presently is 3 years for R&D equipment were even faster; this in turn would enable new firms to have a more rapid recovery of capital costs incurred in production scale-up equipment and would allow an even more rapid recovery of capital costs incurred in production scale-up.

With the present funding and policy issues in biotechnology, the U.S. needs to examine how to cope with the funding needs for long term basic and applied research. Plus the U.S. needs to instigate more indirect means of support by the Federal government that will help universities and private industry, and also develop an effective regulatory policy so that the U.S. can effectively couple potential economic resources in basic and applied research with the development and commercialization of biotechnology.

3

Government/University/Industry Relationships and Interactions

If there continues to be a decline in Federal basic and applied research in the 1980's, universities will increasingly turn to industry for support, and as a result there will be more industrial and university research interaction. If universities do not set realistic future research guidelines, goals and directions in order to maintain their high standards, they may find themselves in the position of doing research solely for financial gains and not for learning and research purposes.

This interaction between academia and industry has developed for several reasons. Today's products, process improvements, and innovations in some industries have evolved to such levels of complexity that they demand an understanding of fundamental physical and biological phenomena, and therefore a much higher level of training is required in the basic sciences and engineering. Also today with the broad range of science and engineering disciplines, it is becoming increasingly difficult for any one industrial laboratory to fully encompass the needed expertise and therefore they turn to universities.

Additionally, the rapid expansion of the nation's R&D system over the past three decades has diffused research capabilities over a much broader range of institutions both academic and industrial. Therefore, it is almost impossible for any one company to maintain a lead on any one technological advance.

In order to deal with this increased industrial/university interaction, universities must understand and deal with retraining scientists, try to deal with the issue of scientists leaving universities for industry, and at the same time they also have to develop policies in regard to the issues of intellectual property rights, and university/industry conflicts of interest.

Universities have to retrain scientists in order to work with the interdisciplinary needs in the biotechnology field. Interdisciplinary basic research on plant biochemistry, development and physiology will be required to help identify important genetic traits and to define biosynthetic pathways in plants. Increased training of students and inducements for scientists from other disciplines will be required to increase the number of people providing basic information on plant properties.

More interest and slightly larger funding levels due to increases in funding in the private sector has spurred activity in addressing the interdisciplinary needs in this field. There is continued high interest in plant biology at the undergraduate, graduate, and postgraduate levels. Highly skilled personnel in advanced areas in genetics have entered into the more traditional botanical laboratories and this combination has provided an excellent means for technology transfer. This is necessary since few traditional botanists have the training in microbiology to set up successful procedures in cloning experiments.

At this time there is a higher concentration of molecular biologists in private universities than in state universities and colleges, since few land grant colleges have recruited personnel in the areas of tissue culture and plant molecular biology. So therefore in private universities there are more opportunities for students to work in several disciplines by simply transferring to laboratories already established on their campus. Additionally there is generally more financial support at private schools with a higher ratio of available predoctoral and postdoctoral opportunities in the laboratories.

Postdoctoral programs in plant molecular biology also help in technology transfer. For instance Duke University, North Carolina State University, and the University of North Carolina at Chapel Hill have formed the triangle universities consortium for research and education in plant molecular biology. The consortium has developed a fellowship program to support the training of graduate students and postdoctoral fellows in both plant science and molecular biology. The Federal government also supports postdoctoral research fellowships in plant biology. For instance the National Science Foundation in the Division of Physiology, Cellular and Molecular Biology is continuing a special program in plant biology. These fellowships provide opportunities for plant scientists to learn the concepts and techniques in other scientific fields in order to approach the problems of plant biology.

Another very important problem that universities have to address today concerns the issue of scientists leaving to find opportunities in private industry since there is a rapid movement of university personnel in that direction. Recruitment efforts by private industry have been highly successful since industry is willing to pay good salaries for a person with a particularly desirable background. Private companies are also able to provide a higher level of research funding, freedom in a research situation, and skilled technical support.

Another obstacle that hinders university/industry relationships concerns the matter of protecting intellectual property. Scientists in universities have a tradition of open communication and are mainly interested in fundamental knowledge with potential applications.

Industry on the other hand is geared to applying knowledge and is primarily interested in the profit picture and the return on any investment in research. This factor understandably makes industry very protective of any forthcoming inventions or patents as compared to public universities who do not always share this concern. Some universities allow the faculty member who developed the invention to retain any patent rights, while some require those rights to be transferred to the institution.

Government grants and contracts give the inventing organization the right to retain title to the invention and allow exclusive licenses under those circumstances. However when universities deal with corporations, this issue is not as clear cut, but most universities will agree that if a faculty member's research is being sponsored by a company in which the faculty member has a substantial interest, the university should grant only a nonexclusive license. However in some agreements exclusive rights have been granted to one corporation.

Another problem in dealing with intellectual property rights concerns the dissemination of the tangible products of research results, which can include antibody-producing cell lines and plasmids used in biotechnology. This is still a major issue in joint agreements between universities and industry that do research and promote advances in genetic engineering. There have been several cases and disputes involving products arising from work conducted at universities, and it is important that there be specific policies developed in order to handle tangible research property.

Conflicts of interest can also develop easily with cooperative agreements. They can arise if a university holds equity in a company in which a faculty member of the university also has equity interest as a line officer, and also can arise when a professor holds equity within a company that engages in the same type of projects as the university. Additionally if a professor is working on a profitable industrial project, this may also cause neglect in the laboratory and classroom. So it is important for universities to be explicit in their conflict of interest and consulting policies.

BIOTECHNOLOGY CENTERS

Since the interdisciplinary nature of biotechnology requires interaction among people with backgrounds in biology and engineering, several biotechnology centers have been created in which the faculty in both biology and engineering are located in the same physical structure and work on common research projects, and work with joint funding from government and industry. Some of these biotechnology centers are as follows:

A) The Center For Innovative Technology (CIT)-- This center was created in 1983 to be run by state universities in conjunction with high technology firms and will bridge the gap between the transfer of scientific discovery from university laboratories to industrial applications. Initially, CIT will focus on research in biotechnology, computer-aided engineering, information technology, and material sciences, but will also insure that Virginia's universities and colleges meet the research needs of industry in other disciplines. CIT will also assist in the development of emerging technically based concerns, assisting

Virginia's universities and colleges in meeting the part-time graduate education needs of industry, and providing services to industry such as a technical resources data bank.

B) Center For Advanced Research In Biotechnology-- Plans are underway for one of four separate institutes to be located in the Shady Grove Life Sciences Center in Gaithersburg Maryland. This center is orientated toward advanced technologies in life sciences and will provide a forum for research activities in molecular biology with emphasis on the manipulation of gene cells.

The center with an initial budget of $1.4 million will use the resources of the University of Maryland, National Bureau of Standards, and private industry in cooperation with the Montgomery County government. The Maryland Biotechnology Institute through CARB will do marine biology and agricultural research and combine the theoretical aspects of biotechnology with practical applications.

C) Michigan Biotechnology Institute--The institute encourages private sector enterprises in the field of applied biology, helps to establish new companies, and strengthens the resources of firms in the field of biotechnology. Its R&D efforts are targeted to fermentation products, and materials from biomass, bioprocessing catalysts, waste treatment bioprocessing equipment, biomass productivity and processing. The institute obtained start-up funding through an Economic Development Authority grant for $6 million and has obtained a grant for $20 million from the Kellogg Foundation.

D) Indiana Corporation For Science & Technology--This
organization is a consortium between the private/industry/public
and academic sectors. The funding is for application-orientated
research that must lead to some product, process, service or other
marketable item. Small amounts of funding for a few small
projects in the biotechnology field have been alloted to the center.

E) Ohio Research and Development Center at Ohio
State--This center has joined with industry to do research on
basic and biotechnology and they are presently studying the impact
of biotechnology on the agricultural systems of the less developed
nations.

F) Cornell Biotechnology Program--The Biotechnology
Institute and the New York State Center For Biotechnology are two
components of this program. The Institute was formed by a joint
effort between the University and several corporations.

So far, three corporations (Eastman Kodak, General Foods,
and Union Carbide) have agreeded to participate in the institute.
Each of these corporations has pledged $2.5 million over a six year
period along with Corning Glass Works who has also made a
substantial contribution to the institute.The institute carries out
basic research and trains scientists in a multi-disciplinary
setting, with the research program focusing on molecular
genetics, cell biology, and cell production.

The New York State Center For Biotechnology is developing
an interdisciplinary program to deal with the basic discoveries in

biology in order to try to solve problems in this field. The center is creating educational and training programs that hopefully will transfer information from the science community to industry, and the center is also monitoring the economic impacts of biotechnology research and development on the state.

(G) North Carolina Biotechnology Center--The center is working with universities, Research Triangle Institute, and industry in order to develop collaborative research and education programs addressing the biomedical, agricultural,and engineering applications of biotechnology.

A working group is designing a biotechnology pilot plant facility to be used by researchers in universities and industry to investigate scale-up problems associated with new biotechnological processes.

The center has published its first comprehensive inventory of biotechnology researchers in North Carolina. The inventory lists researchers, their fields of expertise and areas of study, and is indexed by research field, organisms studies, techniques used, and potential applications.

H) Ben Franklin Partnership Program of Pa.-Much of Pennsylvania's state supported research and development activity is conducted within this program, with a total budget in 1985 of $73 million. This program emphasizes the adaptation of scientific research to the commercial marketplace through the joint involvement of private, academic, and state sectors. Operating through four Advanced Technology Centers, the Ben Franklin Partnership focuses on joint research and development that is of interest to the private sector. They are also involved in entrepreneurial development that includes providing services such as obtaining venture capital, and providing business planning advice.

I) Plant Gene Expression Center--The center was established with the University of California at Berkeley and the California Agricultural Experiment Station with the Center to be located at the ARS Western Regional Research Center in Albany California. The center will assemble experts in genetic engineering to unravel the complex biology of plant gene expression, and to stimulate and coordinate complementary research among public and private research groups.

J) National Science Foundation Industry/University Cooperative Research Centers--These centers promote long-term collaboration between universities and industry on research of mutual interest. Joint support from NSF and industry in starting a center produces a broad-based program that is large enough to be of interest to industry, but often too large for any one company to undertake alone, and therefore this joint effort develops an interdisciplinary program to meet industry's research needs.

There are also several university/industry partnerships that have developed in the biotechnology field that are of benefit to both parties. For instance Agrigenetics formed a limited partnership to attract capital in 1981. This partnership has contracts with several dozen university research workers and their institutions. Patents resulting from the sponsored research belongs to Agrigenetics and in this way the investment fund can be expensed as an R&D investment by the partners. About $55 million was raised and approximately one-half will fund Agrigenetics own in-house research program, the other half will be dispersed to a number of U.S. and foreign institutions. University Genetics, a subsidiary of University Patents, conducts direct non-exclusive relationships with other universities to focus on research programs in biomass and agriculture. Monsanto has a contract with the Rockefeller Foundation to spend $4 million dollars over 5 years to study plant molecular biology. Lastly, Advanced Genetics has an agreement with the University of California to work on research relating to the effects of PGPR on potatoes, tomatoes, corn, cotton, lettuce, cabbage crops, and studying ice nucleation active bacteria.

4

Intellectual Property Law—Patents

U.S Patent Law is designed to encourage invention by granting inventors a limited property right to their inventions. A U.S. patent gives the inventor the right to exclude all others from making, using, or selling the invention within the U.S. without the inventors consent for 17 years. In return the inventor must make full public disclosure of the invention.

The history of plant patent law goes back to the 1930 Plant Patent Act which allowed patent protection for certain asexually propagated plants. It confers the right on the patent holder to exclude others from asexually reproducing the plant or from using or selling any plants reproduced in that way for 17 years. However, it did not address sexually propagated plants because in that era it was not conceivable that plants could produce a stable line through sexual reproduction.

Therefore in 1970, Congress passed the Plant Variety

Protection Act which provides patent-like protection to new distinct, uniform, and stable varieties of plants that are reproduced sexually excluding fungi bacteria and first generation hybrids. The breeder may exclude others from selling, offering for sale, reproducing, importing or exporting the protected variety. Additionally others cannot use it to produce a hybrid or a different variety for sale. However saving seeds for crop production and for the use and reproduction of protected varieties for research is permitted. The period of exclusion is 18 years for woody plants and 17 years for other varieties.

The benefit to farmers under the Plant Variety Protection Act offers a much wider choice of varieties in important crop species because there is more cross breeding efforts, which in turn has increased productivity and improved the consistency of yield by broadening the genetic background of varieties planted by farmers.

The policy of the U.S. Patent and Trademark Office (PTO) has been to allow patent protection for processes using micro-organisms for products containing micro-organisms in combination with inert carriers or other elements, however, the PTO had not issued patents which claimed micro-organisms, per se. The PTO felt that new life forms were not statutory subject matter, and that only legislative action such as the Plant Patent Act of 1930 and the Plant Variety Protection Act of 1970, would permit enlarging the scope of patent protection.

In 1972, Chakrabarty, a microbiologist working for the General Electric Company filed a patent application claiming "a bacterium from the genus Pseudomonas containing at least two stable energy-generating plasmids which provides a separate hydrocarbon degradative pathway." This human-made genetically engineered bacterium was described as capable of breaking down multiple components of crude oil. Because this property is possessed by no naturally occurring bacteria, Chakrabarty believed his invention to have significant value for the treatment of oil spills.

Three categories were involved in the Chakrabarty case 1) the method of producing the bacteria, 2) the bacteria combined with a carrier material and 3) the bacteria themselves. The patent examiner allowed the claims falling into the first two categories, but rejected claims for the bacteria. He based his decision on two grounds-- that micro-organisms are "products of nature" and that as living things they are not patentable subject matter.

Chakrabarty appealed the rejection of these claims to the Patent Office Board of Appeals. The Board reversed the Examiner on the first ground, concluding that the new bacteria were not products of nature because Pseudomonas bacteria contain two or more different energy-generating plasmids, and are not naturally occurring, however they were in agreement on the second ground of rejection. Relying on the legislative history of the 1930 Plant Patent Act, the Board concluded that this does not cover living things such as laboratory created micro-organisms.

Chakrabarty then appealed to the Court of Customs and Patent Appeals where by a divided vote, the decision was reversed and then the case was appealed to the Supreme Court, which held that a live human-made micro-organism is patentable subject matter. After this decision, the PTO issued an announcement that patent applications including claims to micro-organisms which had been under suspension would now be examined.

Presently a company can choose between using patent or trade secret protection. To some companies there are certain advantages in using trade secret protection over patent protection, since a company does not have to reveal information and the protection lasts forever, but this applies only if the trade secret does not become public information.

Patents appear to be the way most companies wish to handle protecting biotechnology. The Patent Office estimates that there are currently 500 genetic manipulation related patent applications pending, and that the office is receiving applications at the rate of 200 per year and this rate is expected to increase.

U.S. and foreign companies are also filing foreign patent applications, but the patent laws of foreign countries differ from those of the U.S. as to the patentability of products and processes. For instance in European countries at the present time new plant varieties cannot be patented. However the Organization For Economic Cooperation And Development has recommended that patent protection in biotechnology research be increased and strengthened. This organization recently published a report entitled *Biotechnology And Patent Protection.*

Presently the U.S. government offers assistance to industry by studying trends in Biotechnology patenting activity through it's Office of Technology Assessment And Forecast within the Patent and Trademark Office. This office reviews high technology areas that are experiencing high levels of patenting. In 1982 this office published a book entitled *Patent Profiles-Biotechnology Update.* This publication does not include all aspects of technology; it mainly focuses on six particular areas of U.S. patents which relate to enzymes and micro-organisms and their use in the synthesis of certain products and their preparation and/or modifications.

The Federal government also provides use of its patented research through the Patent License Office of the USDA Agricultural Research Service, which publishes a catalog of USDA inventions filed for patent. Many of the 1,200 unexpired patents are available for licensing, but few are in biotechnology as the field is still so new.

In the patent field there are still a number of important problems that relate to genetic engineering that need to be addressed. For instance the statutory requirement of "novelty" signifies that an invention must differ from " prior art" which is already publicly known technology. Therefore if scientists publish their research, this places their invention in the public domain and the question arises if this should stop the patent process for in this situation their invention would no longer be considered novel. However in this situation there is a 1 year grace period between the date of any publication by the inventor and the filing of a patent application and therefore this grace period is conducive to the dissemination of new knowledge, since knowledge pertaining to an invention during this period can be published without foregoing the opportunity to file for a patent.

The "utility" standard is another problem, however, it is not generally a difficult standard for individuals or companies to adhere to in seeking patents. Sometimes results of research on DNA may not meet this standard, but companies and individuals can surmount this problem by describing some practical use of the invention in the patent application.

The "nonobviousness" standard that inventions must meet to qualify for a patent pertains to the degree of difference between the invention and the "prior art". If an invention is obvious at the time it was made to a person with ordinary skill in the relevant field of technology, it is not patentable. In other words a patent should not take something that is already in the public domain, that the public enjoys, as an obvious extension of current knowledge.

In the field of biotechnology the basic techniques are known, however since the field is still a very inexact science, many times the genetic manipulation of genetic material will give unexpected results, so therefore the unexpected or superior nature of the results are sometimes the criteria that is necessary to show "nonobviousness".

The requirement for adequate public disclosure presents probably the most serious problem in the patent field. In exchange for a patent the public is guaranteed the right to the new information. The invention must contain a detailed description along with it to allow others to benefit from the invention. In genetic egineeering many biological inventions cannot always be described adequately in writing. Today patent applications on new micro-organisms or processes involving them, permit the micro-organisms to be placed in culture depositories where they are available to the public.

This question of deposit requirements as it relates to public disclosure should be studied carefully since any valid patent must describe an invention sufficiently in order to enable a person of ordinary skill in that technology to make the invention. There is considerable difference in simply describing an invention and actually giving it to another person. The "know-how" that is associated with the actual making and subsequent perfection of an invention clearly provides the inventor with an advantage over a competitor who must construct the invention from the description in the patent. In a field that is so concerned with secrecy this is an important issue since in the case of micro-organisms the invention must actually be turned over to anyone requesting it.

Enforcement in genetic engineering is even more difficult then in other fields since it involves a number of different processes. The owner of a patent on one of those processes may have no way of knowing whether a product made by a competitor has been made by a different process or by the patent owner's process. Another problem that makes enforcement difficult is that process patents granted in the U.S. may be used in foreign countries to make the same product, and then imported into the U.S.

Although U.S. patents have been issued with respect to genetically engineered organisms, there are still important issues that need to be addressed in order to answer the basic questions that relate to patent protection for genetic engineering processes, products of engineered organisms, and to the non-living components of these engineered organisms.

5

Methods Used for International Biotechnology Transfer

Today there is a great deal of technology transfer taking place in the biotechnology field through both official and unofficial channels. While it is important for the U.S. to remain a leader in biotechnology, it is also important to emphasize the transfer of this knowledge to other countries. Some of the methods enabling this diffusion of technical knowledge to other countries include the following:

A) Licensing agreements and joint ventures- These agreements are presently one of the most important ways that biotechnology firms participate in technology transfer, since licensing involves making U.S. firms' patents, trademarks, "know-how" and intellectual property available to individuals and firms in other countries for compensation. Patents arising from these licensing agreements in foreign countries also help to diffuse the technology. New biotechnology firms very often are involved in licensing agreements, since they are not in a financial position to manufacture overseas or to export products from the U.S. Generally these firms have made licensing agreements with foreign companies, or they have invested in a foreign manufacturing subsidiary, or they are involved in joint ventures.

Joint ventures involve actual equity participation by a U.S. company in an overseas operation which is producing the product or utilizing the technology. However, a possible mixed version of a joint venture can involve both a direct capital outlay by the U.S. company to the venture, and a licensing of the U.S. company's technology or "know-how" to the joint venture. In this case there is a pooling of resources and expertise that offsets the high cost of a foreign investment, and additionally there are generally less political and financial risks in joint ventures.

The U.S Export Control regulations are of concern not only to biotechnology companies that presently participate in licensing and joint ventures but also to companies that will be involved in technology transfer and exportation of biotechology products. The Reagan administration is moving to restrict biotechnology exports to the Soviet bloc in order to prevent exports from being used for biological warfare. The U.S. Department of Commerce is drafting new export regulations that would limit biotechnology exports not only to Eastern bloc countries but perhaps even to Europe and Japan. Presently, exporters need either a general license which does not require specific license documents or a validated export license which is required for reasons of national security, short supply, or foreign policy. Items requiring a validated license include certain chemicals, special types of plastics, high technology equipment, scarce materials, and related technical data.

In order to determine whether a validated license is required, it is necessary to consult the Export Administration Regulations and the Commodity Control List. This list may change as the Coordinating Committee for Multilateral Export Controls is studying the need to restrict specific genetic engineering technologies. Today the Commodity Control List include viruses and bacteria. Presently, micro-organisms require a validated license when the micro-organisms are inactivated, attenuated, or fall within Interpretation No. 28 under Commodity Controls. The other commodities that include rDNA and related compounds, and seeds, require a validated license to only two countries while herbicides require a validated license to all countries except Canada.

Aside from the licensing issue there are a number of other trade laws and barriers that are of concern to exporters, but presently there are no unique trade issues pertaining specifically to agricultural biotechnology. In the future as more biotechnology companies get into international trade via other methods other than licensing and joint ventures, there will not only be changes in the export control laws that are of importance to genetic engineering but also to the other scientific disciplines as well.

 B) U.S. International Cooperative Agreements With Foreign Countries--The Office of International Cooperation and Development (OICD) within USDA plans and directs efforts in international development, technology cooperation, and cooperative research in food and agriculture. OICD also develops scientific exchange programs, and works closely with the U.S. and international organizations to assist them in utilizing the scientific resources of the U.S. in order to help other nations.

Some of OICD scientific exchanges and agreements include:

--Bilateral Collaborative Research-Two years ago OICD organized a program of collaborative research involving eminent U.S. and foreign agricultural research centers. Eleven projects involved USDA/ARS laboratories, U.S. agricultural universities, and institutions in Brazil, Mexico, Peru, the Netherlands, West Germany, Australia, and New Zealand.

--U.S. Israel Binational Agricultural Research and Development Fund- This fund was established in October 1977 by the U.S. and Israel as an independent body governed by a board of three American and three Israeli directors and has funded over 240 joint U.S. Israeli research projects.

--Special Foreign Currency Research Program(SFC)-USDA uses foreign currencies to support agricultural and forestry research on problems of mutual interest to the U.S. and participating foreign countries. Since the program began in 1958,

USDA has negotiated over 1,800 projects in 32 nations. During FY 1983 approximately 95 research proposals were approved for negotiation and subsequent funding from SFC or U.S. Yugoslavia Joint Board resources. These proposals were in the areas of basic research, plant germplasm collections and evaluation, human nutrition, hardwood forestry management, and forestry plantations for energy utilization. As a result of this program, there was development of effective control methods for the corn cyst nematode in Egypt with additional research underway in India.

--U.S. Spain Program of Agricultural Research-The 1976 U.S. Spain Treaty of Friendship and Cooperation authorized a program of agricultural research which OICD managed. Funded by the State Department, this program ended in March 1983, but a replacement agreement is now pending. The new program will emphasize basic plant science, animal production and health, forestry, agricultural economics, and technical innovation.

--University Linkages-OICD encourages the participation of U.S. colleges and universities in international research activities with the aim of initiating consultations in areas of mutual concern, and developing proposals for joint research activities. Since the program's inception in FY 1980, awards have been made to eleven U.S. universities and counterpart institutions in Brazil, Colombia, Mexico, Nigeria, and the People's Republic of China.

--Soybean Symposium In China-The second joint U.S.-China

soybean symposium was held in Jilin Province and included U.S. scientific, university, and private agribusiness participants that reviewed progress in soybean research and production and agreed to exchange several germplasm varieties. The Chinese have for the first time provided ten varieties of rare wild germplasm, which may be used to develop new higher yielding U.S. soybean varieties with increased disease resistance.

--Air Pollutant Injury To Crops (France)-Increased use of coal for power generation has exposed major agronomic areas of the U.S. to higher levels of air pollution. Estimated annual economic losses from sulfur and nitrogen oxide damage to animal and plant life range from $1.7 to $9 billion dollars. American and French scientists are studying selected crop species reactions to the presence of sulfur dioxide and the differences in crop resistance to environmental stress. This information is essential to the development of hardier species and successful breeding in pollution prone areas.

--Biocontrol of Grasshoppers (Australia)-Grasshoppers have caused an average of $23 million dollars in damage in the Great Plains each year for the past 25 years. Exchanges of information with Australian experts will center on studying biological control using new techniques in isolating pathogens that have been developed in the past 2 years.

The National Science Foundation also supports several cooperative science programs. One such agreement between NSF and the Japan Society For The Promotion Of Science studied the natural sciences. In this agreement there were several biotechnology projects that applied to plant agriculture. One project studied the chemical control of flowering in the Lemnaceae. The main purpose was to better understand the chemical control of flowering and the Lemnaceae by doing chemical analyses of the extract from the plant Lemna gibba G3 and the plant Lemna paucicostala 381.

Another project studied the regulation of nitrogen metabolism in plants. The objective was to elucidate interaction and regulatory mechanisms of nitrogen carbon metabolism, and to obtain fundamental knowledge for improvement of plant productivity. Studies were done on the overall regulation of nitrogen assimilation, the interaction of nitrogen and photosynthesis, the regulation of nitrogen assimilation in light and dark, regulation of photosynthesis in relation to nitrogen assimilation, and lastly, on developing specific mutants to aid in regulation studies.

Another project studied nitrogen fixation in soybeans. The objective of this project was to elucidate the physiological and microbiological problem related to soybean plant production, including such aspects as the quality and quantity of carbohydrates supplied to nitrogen fixing nodules, translocation, transformation and accumulation of nitrogenous compounds and selection of appropriate root nodule bacteria.

The National Science Foundation supports some other projects. One project involves a U.S. and U.K. seminar on plant mitochondrial DNA research. Another project underway between the University of Oxford and the University of Massachusetts focuses on defining the molecular basis of protein maturation in yeast by means of genetic engineering. The results of this research will lead to a better understanding of protein secretion in yeast. Additionally, NSF supports another cooperative project with Switzerland to study the use of immobilized plant cell cultures to produce various biochemicals in a convenient continuous way. Certain plants produce compounds, such as pharmaceuticals, agrichemicals, enzymes, and other substances that have not yet been synthesized in the laboratory and are not practical to synthesize on a large scale. By culturing the appropriate plant cells and adjusting conditions properly, it is possible to exploit in a convenient controlled manner the natural biosynthetic processes occurring in these plants. This technique will permit biotransformation of certain low cost substances to valuable plant compounds. The culturing and immobilization of plant cells are analogous to similar procedures that have been applied to microbial cells, but important differences require that new techniques be developed.

The Agency For International Development (AID) is placing a new emphasis on science and technology. The Science and Technology Bureau within AID has undertaken a number of cooperative programs between AID and U.S. universities, since the Foreign Assistance Act calls for U.S. land grant colleges and universities and other institutions which include USDA to be involved in international food and agricultural development.

AID has provided 25% of the core budget for the 13 centers sponsored by The Consultative Group on International Agricultural Research (CGIAR). This group is also sponsored by representatives of government, regional banks, the World Bank and a number of international and bilateral agencies, multilateral donors, and foundations.

These 13 centers work effectively with national programs in providing germplasm, training researchers and providing advice and networking. AID and the World Bank supplement these activities by giving funds to help improve national agricultural research. Results from this program have enabled India and Pakistan to triple their wheat production with the introduction of dwarf wheat, South Korea has greatly improved their rice production, Indonesia has developed new research capabilities, and Asia has made great gains in agriculture. In the 1990's, scientists feel that there will be a significant increase in sorghum production since a new sorghum germplasm has been developed to improve yields.

AID also funded a workshop on Priorities in Biotechnology Research For International Development which was organized by the National Academy of Sciences to discuss research that would help crop production and energy sources. Other workships have been sponsored to discuss how to increase crops in developing countries.

In the 1980's, AID plans to set new priorities to develop a research agenda on food and agriculture that will take place in developing countries and in turn these countries and scientific organization will share biotechnology research and research accomplishments with other developing countries.

C) Other Methods For International Technology Transfer--There are of course additional ways in which governments and private companies provide technology transfer. Scientists are publishing their research results at international seminars and workshops, scientists are constantly corresponding and exchanging specimens, and private consulting agreements are being initiated between firms and universities that are interested in participating in technology transfer projects.

In future agricultural technology transfer ventures, the U.S. and other countries will initiate new agricultural training programs, new cooperative agricultural research projects between countries with high technology resources and developing countries, set up international germplasm collections and specimen exchanges, and develop and share our knowledge in order to produce better methods for crop forecasting and production. All of these methods will produce more food world-wide and perhaps this will make countries more stable and produce economically sound economies that in turn will become markets for our agricultural supplies and equipment.

6

Regulatory Options

Industry understands that Federal regulation of the biotechnology industry is inevitable and will come within the near future. The main question at this point is what agency or agencies should be entrusted with this regulatory power. Efforts presently are underway to regulate and coordinate research activities, and biotechnology products within these particular agencies and committees:

1) NIH Recombinant DNA Advisory Committee (RAC)--Monitors certain biotechnology research and approves all experiments on genetically engineered organisms within the public sector.

2) Food and Drug Administration--Regulates new drugs and the FDA Recombinant DNA Coordinating Committee sets biotechnology policies within FDA.

3) USDA Recombinant DNA Advisory Committee--

Identifies issues with regard to rDNA research and application activites, and makes recommendations. The committee also provides input and assistance to the USDA representative to the NIH Recombinant DNA Advisory Committee and additionally serves as the USDA information clearinghouse on scientific research in this field.

4) Environmental Protection Agency--Presently, the Toxic Substances Control Act (TSCA) authorizes EPA to acquire information on chemical substances in order to evaluate potential hazards, and the Federal Insecticides Fungicide and Rodenticide Act (FIFRA) has jurisdiction over pesticides and health and environmental effects.

5) The Occupational Safety and Health Administration and the National Institute of Occupational Safety--OSHA and NIOSH are concerned with the welfare of biotechnology employees.

Other committees that are involved in regulatory issues include the Interagency Risk Management Committee initiated in 1984, and the White House Office of Science Technology and Policy's Cabinet Council Working Group, and the Interagency Committee on Food, Agriculture and Forestry Research.

This decision as to what agency or agencies will eventually be responsible for regulatory matters is of concern to both large and small companies in the industry. No one in the industry wants to get bogged down in rules and red tape in an industry that is just beginning to make important advances.

Presently just trying to learn who regulates what is a frustrating and costly undertaking for many companies. Products of biotechnology are already within the domain of EPA and FDA, but the conflict for regulation of products that will be environmentally released has not been determined.

Industry of course realizes that there are many dangers associated with the release of genetically manipulated organisms into the environment, however this uncertainty about the Federal government's authority to regulate activities may affect such activities as the use of microbial enhanced oil recovery, pollution control, mineral leaching and the genetic manipulation of plants. Not only is the biotechnology industry concerned about regulatory issues in the U.S. but they are also forced to consider the complications of overseas business and how the U.S regulatory stand will affect international biotechnology commercialization.

Presently there are several proposed regulatory options under consideration such as:

1) EPA could have regulatory powers under the Toxic Substances Control Act and the Federal Insecticides Fungicide and Rodenticide Act (FIFRA). However, it is not clear whether micro-organisms are chemical substances under TSCA, whether regulations focus on rDNA molecules rather than the organisms containing them, whether genetically engineered organisms are new chemicals under TSCA, and lastly can TSCA be applied to research activities and field trials. Under FIFRA, it has not been

determined whether data should be required on each genetic isolate of an engineered organism. These questions must be answered if EPA is to have regulatory powers under TSCA and FIFRA. Large companies support regulatory functions within EPA since they feel that EPA has regulatory experience and also large organizations have the expertise to deal with the red tape of Federal agencies. Other companies however feel that there will be a problem if EPA concentrates too heavily on rDNA while ignoring the other forms of biotechnology.

2) Presently the NIH Recombinant DNA Committee studies all proposals for rDNA but is only involved in experiments involving potent biological toxins. Some companies feel that NIH does not have enough regulatory experience, but they like the committee's control of non-governmental rDNA research, since in these cases the committee responds quickly and has the flexibility to deal with research and experimentation. However even though the committee is held in high esteem, it is sometimes felt that the committee does not have enough power and sometimes appears as an adjunct of NIH.

3) FDA already has regulatory powers over new products seeking food processing or medical applications. FDA's system for reviewing genetically engineered products and monoclonal antibodies technology is generally highly considered by the industry. However questions have to be answered as to whether each genetically engineered product be tested on a case by case

basis, and also how will new genetically engineered foods be monitored for active biological substances.

4) Under USDA most of the agricultural products presently produced will fit into the agencies existing legislation except for plant seeds developed through recombinant techniques. USDA will also have to approve micro-organisms that may be introduced into the environment differently and make new decisions on new types of herbicides.

5)The National Environmental Protection Act requires an environmental impact statement for any major federal action. The industry is fearful of being subject to this act as many feel that this could play havoc with the emerging biotechnology industry.

6)Legislation could be passed on recombinant DNA. Some members of the industry feel that the legislation passed would be too specialized and would not serve the needs of the industry.

7) A Congressional watchdog is a possibility. Opponents feel that this might create more government and open another regulatory government agency which at this point draws almost no support from the industry.

8) The laboratory level of the Federal agencies could possibly regulate the industry. The industry is concerned that research laboratories with several programs in pharmaceuticals, specialty chemicals and agriculture would have several agencies overseeing experimentation and research.

9) State laws could possibly be enacted to regulate the

industry. The industry fears that several guidelines might exist for genetically engineered organisms within different state legislations and therefore is considered by the industry as most ineffective.

In response to the many possibilities and difficulties involved in the area of regulatory authority, the White House in January of 1985, proposed the formation of a Biotechnology Science Board that would oversee genetic engineering and create advisory committees at FDA, USDA, EPA, and NSF similar to NIH's recombinant DNA advisory committee. If this board were created the NIH recombinant DNA advisory committee would find its responsibilities and scope limited. Due to opposition to the Biotechnology Science Board a proposal is now under consideration for a biotechnology coordinating committee that would be chaired alternately by the directors of NIH and NSF. This proposed board would operate as an interagency coordinating council and be chartered out of the White House Office of Science Technology and Policy.

There is much debate in the industry on this issue as to which options should be considered and this uncertainty over the Federal government's regulatory stand over the industry makes it difficult for companies to plan research and produce biotechnology products. The industry is seeking a rational regulatory approach that will be sensitive to the problems of all biotechnology firms.

Part II

Overview of Federal Biotechnology Activities

7

Activities Within the Federal Agencies

The prime responsibility for plant agriculture biotechnology research is conducted within USDA with research programs in the Agricultural Research Service, Cooperative State Research Service, and the Forest Service. Additionally the Office of International Cooperative Development participates in international science exchanges. The USDA programs are as follows:

U.S. DEPARTMENT OF AGRICULTURE

The Agricultural Research Service (ARS) carries out the in-house research on photosynthesis, biological nitrogen fixation, cell cultures, plant stress, and plant growth regulators. The ARS National Program Staff is responsible for research planning, priority setting, program evaluation, and allocation of resources. In this capacity they work with the 11 area administrative directors and report directly to the Administrator of ARS.

ARS also works closely with the State Experimental Stations -- for instance 25 laboratories within the Beltsville Maryland area have formal cooperative agreements with the Maryland Agricultural Experiment Station. ARS also works closely with their overseas laboratories which are involved in research to find environmentally sound alternatives to chemical controls for insects, weeds and other pests.

The Cooperative State Research Service (CSRS), another research arm of USDA, primarily conducts its biotechnology research through the Competitive and previously through the Special Grant research programs conducted at land grant universities and colleges and through the state agricultural experiment stations.

CSRS is organized into units of Plant and Animal Sciences and Natural Resources, Human Nutrition, Food and Social Sciences. In addition to these activities, CSRS has advisory committees such as the Cooperative Forestry Research Advisory Board, the National Plant Genetic Resources Board, and the Aquaculture Advisory Board that provide input on research needs.

The Forest Service also has a genetic engineering research program. Primarily, the research program is performed at eight experimental centers and concentrates on studying the methodologies for transferring genetic information in forest tree species which includes the study of vectors, gene expression and the study of enzyme systems. The program also includes studies on pest resistance, cell fusion, transformation, and tissue cultures.

The Office of International Cooperative Development (OICD) within USDA conducts scientific exchange programs and exchanges research findings on statistics, data and technology. OICD administers a variety of international research projects and in this capacity works closely with scientists in land grant institutions and USDA researchers.

There are several mediating or linking bodies within USDA and these include the Joint Council and Users Advisory Board. They produce annual reports detailing the accomplishments of ongoing research, national policies and priorities and strategies for agricultural research.

Additionally there are other agencies that contribute to biotechnology plant agriculture activities in a number of ways.

These agencies include the National Science Foundation, the Department of Energy, Health and Human Services, Department of Commerce, Environmental Protection Agency, Department of State, Agency For International Development, Small Business Administration, Department of Labor, TVA, the Legislative branch, Congressional Committees, Congressional resources, the Executive Branch, Interagency committees and non-profit organizations and associations.

NATIONAL SCIENCE FOUNDATION

Research supported by NSF in biotechnology will target plant cell protoplast culture, cell fusion and the biochemistry of plant generation, identification and production of active peptides such as neuropeptides and hormones as well as plant cell products which impart natural resistance to insects and disease, and lastly, the development of bioreactors including modern approaches to fermentation technology and methods of product recovery. Additionally the Office of Biotechnology within the Directorate for Biological Behavior and Social Sciences has been established to maintain a biotechnology information system and to examine the potential effects of environmentally related basic research in biotechnology.

Program areas at NSF which presently support biotechnolgy research are as follows:

-Advanced Technologies and Resources Policy program studies the role of the Federal government and the private sector in biotechnology R&D.

-Alternative Biological Resources program supports the development of alternate domestic sources of energy and research to study critical materials of biological origin.

-Automation, Instrumentation and Sensing Systems program contributes to the knowledge base required for an improved understanding of machine systems and automated decision and control techniques in either a physical or biological problem domain.

-Biochemistry program supports research aimed at understanding the molecular basis of life.

-Biological Instrumentation program provides support for proposals from multi-user groups to purchase major research instruments, and it also supports the development of instruments which provide increased capability for measuring the detailed structure, dynamics, interactions and alterations that occur in biological systems.

-Biological Oceanography program in biotechnology relates to the unique physiological and biochemical pathways of organisms which function in the extreme environments of deep sea hydrothermal vents.

-Biophysics program supports research using physical techniques for investigating basic biological phenomena, and research involving physical interactions of macro-molecules with themselves or with their environment.

-Cell Biology program supports research directed toward understanding the mechanisms underlying the growth, division and behavior of prokaryotic and eukaryotic cells in-vivo and in cultures.

-Cellular Physiology program supports research to understand the reception of information by and within cells and the response of cells to that information.

-Chemical Analysis program supports research on new or improved methods to analyze all forms of matter in all media.

-Chemical and Biochemical Processes program supports research on the basic aspects of chemical and biochemical processes in a variety of technological areas.

-Chemical Dynamics program supports research on correlations and generalizations relating molecular structure, energetics and reactivity.

-Chemical Instrumentation program provides funds to assist the scientific community in acquiring multi-user instrumentation essential for conducting research in chemistry

-Developmental Biology program supports research on the development of animals, plants and micro-organisms.

-Ecology program supports research in the ecology of organisms existing in extreme environments.

Genetic Biology program supports research focused on the organization, function, transmission, and regulation of the expression of hereditary material of all organisms as well as their viruses.

The Office of Cross-Disciplinary Research within NSF is the coordinator of the committee of program directors participating in the above programs. This office also has an experimental program in support of research leading to instrumentation in the field of biotechnology. For instance an award was made to the University of Tennessee FY 1984 for $85,000 to perform research on fiberoptics-based fluoroimmuno sensors and another award was made to the University of Pennsylvania FY 1984 for $100,000 to develop pyroelectric based immobilized enzyme sensors.

The Office of Cross-Disciplinary Research also sponsors workshops with other organization's support on areas of interest in biotechnolgy and biochemical engineering. In 1984, a conference was held with the University of California at Berkeley on biological control in agricultural IPM systems and another conference was held in 1984 with Battelle on bioprocess scale-up.

DEPARTMENT OF ENERGY

The Department of Energy is involved in research on Biochemical and Photobiological Conversion Research through the Office of Renewable Technology, Division of Biomass Energy Technology.

Biochemical conversion via anaerobic digestion involves the controlled decomposition of biomass by micro-organisms. Research is being performed on the microbiology and biochemistry of digestion cultures and on the genetic manipulation of bacteria in the methane production cycle for increased methane yields and biomass conversion efficiencies.

Hydrogen can be used as a feedstock for synthetic fuel production or can be directly combusted. Fundamental research covers production of hydrogen using photosynthetic bacteria and algae. Studies with algae encompass methods for improving the algae's ability to split water into hydrogen and oxygen. Oxygen production is an important initial phase in the production of hydrogen from water. DOE research in this area also includes the experimental evaluation on in-vitro cell-free concepts.

These concepts are expected to make use of photochemically active portions of the cell's photosynthetic apparatus, which are removed from the cell to yield a water-splitting capability. Theory predicts that hydrogen production efficiency will be higher for in-vitro, cell-free processes than for those involving whole-cell micro-organisms.

The biomass program has a new genetics program to develop wood resources with high yields, to improve resistance to pests and disease, and to lower nitrogen or water requirements. Additionally, research will be conducted to improve the oil content, increase growth rates, and to determine methods for harvesting microalgae as an energy resource.

The Office of Energy Research in their Basic Energy Sciences Program is involved in biological research to study the transfer of pieces of DNA into host plants without causing the development of tumors in those plants and therefore introduce desirable traits into plants to improve plant species for the production of biomass.

DEPARTMENT OF HEALTH AND HUMAN SERVICES

The Food and Drug Administration is concerned with the safety factors in agricultural biotechnology as it concerns the use of micro-organisms, plant cells, or parts of cells, to produce commercial quantities of useful substances. The agency is involved in the safety of products resulting from research and is involved with several interagency coordinating committees.

The National Institutes of Health is involved in biotechnology policy and regulatory issues and supports some limited areas of plant research but this research is essentially initiated by individual investigators. The Center For Disease Control and the National Institute of Occupational Safety and Health along with OSHA at the Department of Labor are involved in developing safety guidelines for workers who create industrial applications of recombinant DNA.

DEPARTMENT OF COMMERCE

The National Bureau of Standards within the Department of Commerce, provides industry with data and measurement methods for processing materials, quality assurance and control. Since biotechnology is a branch of molecular biology, it requires development of measurement methods related to biologically active molecules. The National Bureau of Standards works cooperatively with the University of Maryland in biotechnology efforts and also sponsors a series of biotechnology seminars.

The Patent & Trademark Office within the Department of Commerce is responsible for novel micro-organisms that are patentable and they have also done biotechnology patent profiles.

The International Trade Administration within the Department of Commerce is knowledgeable on foreign countries and scientific activities as it relates to plant agriculture and food production.

Lastly the National Technical Information Service has full

summaries of Federal government research reports in hundreds of subject categories, and this information is disseminated through newsletters, and in other subscription formats.

ENVIRONMENTAL PROTECTION AGENCY

The Office of Research and Development (ORD) obtains research guidance on biotechnology as it relates to the environment. ORD is researching the survival of organisms that change genetically, studying the possibility of novel organisms escaping from containment, and also researching the exchange and transfer of genetic information and how this will relate to the environment.

The Office of Toxic Substances (OTS) is working on regulatory mechanisms in order to work with products produced by genetic engineering that in some way could possibly affect the environment. OTS through the Premanufacturing Notification (PMN) process reviews new chemical substances before they are manufactured. It is estimated that in 1985 there will be up to 10 PMN applications in the field of genetic engineering and that OTS will probably review applications on a case by case basis.

The Office of Pesticide Programs (OPP) is expected to handle the submission of genetically engineered microbial pesticides within the next few years and is presently examining additional data requirements that will accompany the registration of these genetically engineered microbial pesticides.

DEPARTMENT OF STATE

The Department of State has the prime responsibility to

understand biotechnology as it affects our relationships with foreign countries and is mostly concerned with technology transfer as it relates to policies and laws that direct the flow of technical data.

In the future, it is anticipated that the Department of State will become more heavily involved in the international political, scientific, and commercial prospects of biotechnology. Although the Department of State is not primarily a research agency, it sponsors some projects through the Agency for International Development (AID) and the Office of Agriculture.

AID presently is involved in agricultural research with U.S land grant colleges and USDA, but there is limited concentration on biotechnology. However the AID Science Advisor Program was established in 1980 to encourage scientific activity in developing countries, and this program supports small grants for research that involve biological and chemical aspects as they relate to agriculture, health, and biomass energy. The Science Advisor Program also coordinates and administers conferences and studies on research topics relating to developing countries. There is also a program that AID and the American Association For the Advancement of Sciences are working on that involves biotechnology applications in third world countries. Additionally, The Office of Agriculture within AID published a report in 1982 outlining the priorities that need to be set in biotechnology research. In the future AID expects to see an increase in research support for food and agriculture and expects to develop specific biotechnology research projects.

The Office of Agriculture within the Department of State's Bureau of International Organization Affairs is primarily concerned with biotechnology as it applies to international development and presently this office serves as the link with the UN agricultural organizations.

SMALL BUSINESS ADMINISTRATION

SBA is involved in the biotechnology through the Small Business Investment Corporations (SBIC) which presently helps small companies raise capital funds. SBICs are private companies licensed by SBA that are required to invest their funds in small businesses. Although some SBICs have invested in new biotechnology firms, SBICs do not generally commit public funds guaranteed by public institutions to high risk ventures like biotechnology.

TENNESSEE VALLEY AUTHORITY

The Tennessee Valley Authority through their Office Of Agriculture and Chemical Development plans and manages programs for demonstration of new and improved agricultural methods.

LEGISLATIVE BRANCH

The legislative branch has a number of committees with jurisdiction over agricultural policy and budgets. These include the House and Senate Budget Committees, the House and Senate

Appropriations Committees, the House and Senate Committee on Agriculture, the Senate Committee on Nutrition and Forestry, Senate Committee on Commerce, Senate Committee on Science, and Transportation, and the House Committee on Science and Technology. The House and Senate Committees also obtain information on agricultural priorities and budgets from the Congressional Budget Office, the Congressional Research Service, the General Accounting Office, and the Office of Technology Assessment (OTA). OTA has an office for biological applications and published a report in January 1984 entitled *Commercial Biotechnology: An International Analysis*.

EXECUTIVE BRANCH

The Executive Branch of the Federal government also plays a key role in policy and information. The Office of Management and Budget addresses the budgetary aspects of agricultural research while the Office of Science Technology Policy within the Executive Office of the President addresses issues of national priorities that include genetic engineering and the many issues and policies that will have to address biotechnology in the future.

INTERAGENCY COMMITTEES AND COORDINATION

There are a number of interagency committees that are involved in biotechnology and have been established to coordinate policy, and to share information within the agencies involved in genetic engineering. These committees include the following:

-NIH Recombinant DNA Advisory Committee and the Office

of Recombinant DNA Activities serve as a clearinghouse and provides information to other agencies.

-Agricultural Recombinant DNA Advisory Committee has recently been involved with setting new guidelines and policies of its own for USDA applications. In the future it is anticipated that this committee will gain prominence as the advisory body responsible for agricultural related biotechnology research.

-Office Of Science Technology Policy (OSTP) Committee on Food, Agriculture and Forest Research is a high level effort to study what agricultural research each agency is participating in and to address some of the policy issues. Agencies represented include USDA, NSF, NIH, DOE, Department of State, Department of Interior, TVA.

-OSTP Cabinet Council Working Group on Biotechnology was formed to review federal agency activities on biotechnology.

-OSTP Interagency Working Group on Competitive and Transfer Aspects of Biotechnology studies the transfer of technology abroad.

-Interagency Risk Management Council was formed to coordinate regulatory policies in biotechnology and agencies represented include EPA, USDA, Department of Labor, and Health and Human Services.

Other informal groups include a working group initiated by the Office of Naval Research to promote information among agencies and the National Science Foundation also has an interagency committee on plant biology.

ASSOCIATIONS

The associations that make important contributions on the needs of biotechnology research to the legislative and executive bodies of government include the American Association for the Advancement of Science, National Academy of Sciences, National Association of Universities and Land Grant Colleges, the Industrial Biotechnology Association, and the Association of Biotechnology Companies.

These are the Federal agencies, the Congressional committees, interagency committees and boards, and private sector associations and organizations that provide input into the many inherent problems in the field of genetic engineering. There of course needs to be a great deal of input into these problems, but better coordination is needed not only between Federal agencies involved in biotechnology, but also between all branches of government.

In the meantime a number of knowledgeable individuals in the public and private sector feel that a temporary biotechnology regulatory coordinating committee should be formed that would represent not only food and agriculture, but broader interests and also be responsible for preparing independent advisory opinions on proposed regulations for laboratory and field tests as well as on regulatory guidelines for commercial products.

This committee could also serve in a consulting capacity

to the President; additionally, they could assess the social, ethical, economic, and environmental effects of conducting research, and identify new opportunities or problems related to biotechnology research and development.

Input and coordination through such a mechanism as this proposed committee along with other interagency committees plus input from all branches of government, the private sector, universities, foundations, and associations, are needed in order to have an effective Federal and industrial biotechnology program.

8

Information on Research Within the USDA Agricultural Research Service

AGRICULTURAL RESEARCH SERVICE

The Agricultural Research Service (ARS) is currently working on 200 plant and animal biotechnology research projects. The projects are being conducted in 41 locations, with funding of $15.4 million with a budget at Beltsville Maryland of about $6,260,000 to be spent on new biotechnology research throughout the country. Primarily the Beltsville Agricultural Research Center in Beltsville Maryland does research on plant genetics and genetic engineering, biochemistry, hormones, nitrogen fixation, photosynthesis and stress effects on plant growth and function, while the Western Regional Research Center in Albany California is also concerned with basic and applied research on plant growth, hormones and regulators, nitrogen fixation, and photosynthesis.

Recent ARS research accomplishments:

-Single cells from potato plants that are difficult to cross are being fused to overcome major barriers to breeding better potatoes. A sensitive diagnostic test for the presence of viroids in potatoes has also been devised and is being used in several countries to ensure disease free seed potatoes.

-Scientists working on sugarbeet genes have discovered that establishing gene locations on chromosomes can be done by using trisomic plants--those having a specific extra chromosome.

-A one minute test for rubber, resin, and moisture content of guayule has been developed to replace the current slow tedious process, so that guayule could be a source of domestic rubber.

-In a new automated plant culture system, plants develop twice as fast as with a manual system and this new system has promise for commercial application.

-ARS in cooperation with the States developed two new soybean varieties which are near release for use in northern production areas; both are resistant to race 3 SCN and to several important diseases. Also molecular biochemical techniques have determined that chloroplast DNA is the site that contains information for photosynthesis and this information will be important in breeding programs.

-Scientists are trying to improve the potential for increased crop yields of sugarcane by the use of growth regulating compounds, cell and tissue culture techniques, and improved gene transfer systems. They are also studying the physiological mechanism of sucrose transport by somaclonal variants and this should help to manipulate the plant to produce more sucrose.

-Thousands of cereal grains being grown in field nurseries will undergo a battery of tests aimed at cataloging their characteristics for inclusion in the National Small Grain Collection.

The Agricultural Research Service's main biotechnology emphasis within their 6 year implementation (1984-1990) plan includes the following research agenda at Beltsville Maryland:

--Scientists are researching how to characterize and manipulate biologically important genes and their products. They are using a number of approaches such as identifying the different life forms such as crop plants, seeds, weeds, insects, bacteria, and viruses by their physical characteristics, and work is progressing on developing chromosome handling techniques, studying cytogenetics and examining isozymes.

The scientists are also working on identifying and manipulating the genes in order to convert atmospheric nitrogen into protein and trying to improve the nitrogen fixation process. The researchers are approaching the problem by:

--Identifying the genes involved in nitrogen fixation in legumes, improving them, and then inserting them into grain crops. They are trying to determine the genes controlling the mutual recognition between plant and nitrogen-fixing bacterium. Colonization of the plant nodule by the bacterium should permit enhancement of colonization and improve the growth of plants.

Recombinant DNA methodology is also being used to improve nitrogen fixation ability in legumes and to transfer this ability to grain crops and thereby reduce the need for nitrogen fertilizer.

-- Introducing plasmids into soil bacteria that control the degradation of agricultural pesticides and this should reduce the persistence of pesticides, prevent movement out of the root zone into the ground water, and provide a safe disposal system.

--Characterizing and manipulating the biologically important genes of soil micro-organisms that will provide biological control agents for soilborne diseases and thereby reduce the need for pesticides and increase crop productivity.

--Applying plant cell and tissue culture techniques, such as anther culture and early stage embryo rescue. These techniques will greatly accelerate the development of important economic crops with better resistance to insects and diseases, increase yields, and provide a better balance of nutrients.

--Identifying and understanding the genes that control partition of nutrients and the synthesis of protein in seeds. Once identified, the genes can be altered to increase the amount of nutrients that go to storage organs such as seeds and taproots and therefore increase the protein content of the stored product.

--Developing improved methods for transferring genes from one plant to another, and researchers are using such methods as electrofusion of protoplasts and chromosome-mediated transformation. These techniques will allow the transfer of genetic information from one plant species to another.

--Identifying the genes in micro-organisms that control production of microbial components that trigger resistance in plants. Insertion of these genes into saprophytes will be used as a tool in increasing the resistance of plants to disease agents.

--Identifying, isolating, and characterizing genes in micro-organisms by restriction-endonuclease mapping and hybridization. The organisms studied include arthropod viruses, bacteria that produce arthropod toxins, plant viruses, viroids, bacteriophages, and spiroplasmas. These studies will provide a better understanding of plant pathogens and improved methods of controlling disease organisms, including biocontrol of insects.

--Developing monoclonal antibodies to plant viruses and plant pathogens that will advance studies of pathogen-host interactions, disease expression and control.

--Elucidating the specific gene structure, expression, and molecular mechanisms of the action of germination promoters and inhibitors that will lead to better control and rates of germination.

Scientists at ARS in Beltsville are also working on the structure of plant membranes in order to investigate how herbicides and insecticides affect them, what causes ripening, how to prevent injury to membranes on freezing, and they are studying the unique structures on membranes of parasites. Researchers are studying membranes by using nuclear magnetic resonance, x-ray diffraction, high electron microscopy and a host of other techniques. When scientists study the membrane of the chloroplast, and measure ratios of different types of molecules, they have shown that a series of electron-transfer reactions that convert light energy to chemical energy in plants takes place at sites on the chloroplast membrane. Such energy transfer in crop plants has a direct impact on yield. Scientists are proceeding with membrane research by:

-- Identifying the types of environmental stress that alter membranes biochemically and anatomically in hopes that this will reveal ways of preventing membrane damage due to environmental stress.

--Trying to understand the action of oxidants on plant-membrane antioxidant systems and substituting pyridazinones that alter fatty acid composition of plant membranes. Researchers hope this will permit an improved understanding of how these compounds regulate membrane function. Controlling membrane function will reveal ways to prevent the damaging effects of these compounds on plants.

-- Studying the role of light and other environmental factors on membrane function as mediated by hormones, so that researchers will have a better understanding of how the plant apportions carbohydrates among different organs.

--Studying how controlling photosynthate partitioning and how altering plant hormone control in the transport of metabolites through membranes can enhance crop productivity.

-- Understanding how membranes control penetration, absorption, and translocation of herbicides and bioregulators through themselves and through tissues and plant systems, and how this will allow the development of more effective and specific herbicides and bioregulators.

-Understanding the structure and function of membrane/cell wall components and the genes that control these components is a key step in understanding maturation, ripening, and senescence. Controlling senescence will improve the quality of fruits and vegetables.

Researchers in studying the mechanism of interorgan communications are working to:

--Develop monoclonal antibodies to specific metabolites that will give sensitive probes to identify, localize, and quantify these metabolites in growth, development, and senescence. The researchers are trying to find ways to alter these metabolites which will allow the development of more productive plants.

-- Develop methods for regeneration of plants from tissue culture cells that will permit the application of gene transfer technologies and greatly accelerate plant improvement.

--Measure and understand the mode of the action of plant growth regulators such as brassino-steroids and the use of synthetic substitutes of regulators that will allow the control of plant functions such as germination, flowering, fruit retention, growth, maturation, and senescence. Application of these substances can significantly increase yield, shorten time to harvest, and prevent deterioration after harvest.

A questionnaire was sent out to the research centers to find out the involvement of ARS in biotechnology research. The responses included information on research projects and abstracts from locations throughout the country. Selected ARS research projects involved in biotechnology are included in the following information.

ARS BIOTECHNOLOGY RESEARCH PROJECTS

Researchers at the Food Proteins Research Unit at the ARS Western Regional Research Center in Albany California are working on several projects that involve the wheat plant. Frank Greene is working on 2 research projects.

One is studying <u>molecular control of gene activity during reproductive development in the wheat plant.</u> During development of the wheat seed, genes that control the synthesis of amino acids appear to be expressed in a manner that complements the demands of the protein synthesis system. This suggests that some coordination of gene expression occurs, possibly controlled through structural elements of the genes themselves.

The objective of this project is to determine the prevalence of coordinated gene expression in the developing wheat seed, and to identify the factors that control such expression. The expression of glutamate-oxaloacetate transaminase (GOT), which facilitates the exchange of nitrogen among several amino acids, has been found to be different in seeds and leaves of the wheat plant, with different forms (isozymes) of the enzyme dominant in each tissue.

The dominant GOT seed isozyme follows a pattern of expression similar to that of storage protein genes, and reaches a much higher level of activity than the dominant leaf form. The gene coding the dominant seed isozyme will be isolated, and its potential controlling structures compared to those gliadin genes which have been isolated in the laboratory. These isolated genes will also be used as probes to identify and isolate presumptive gene-activating factors from endosperm cell nuclei. These experiments have the potential for determining the molecular basis for time and tissue-specific gene expression. The researchers feel that such a determination would facilitate the construction of modified genes which would have predictable patterns of expression after insertion into wheat or other host plants.

In another project Frank Greene is studying the genetic aspects and biosynthesis of wheat protein. The genetics and synthesis of wheat seed protein systems is not understood well enough to allow interventions that would significantly improve their quality characteristics.

The objective of this project is to acquire the knowledge necessary to facilitate such improvements via molecular biological approaches. Nuclear DNA has been isolated from several wheat cultivars, cleaved with restriction enzymes, and the chromosomal origin of several gliadin gene containing fragments were determined by hybridization analysis.

DNA from Cheyenne wheat has been cloned in a bacteriophage vector to produce a genetic library which contains cloned copies of probably all the genes of this cultivar. In addition to information that determines protein structures, this cloned library includes regulatory information that determines the pace and pattern of wheat development. The complete nucleotide sequence of the protein-coding region of a cloned gliadin gene, and some of the sequence of the flanking control regions has been determined.

Presently, analysis of the structures of additional genes is underway and experiments on the in-vitro transcription of these genes have been initiated which should allow identification of the critical sequences which control their expression. This information makes it possible to analyze the expression of individual wheat genes in the laboratory, to identify the critical DNA sequences which control their expression, and to facilitate the transfer of genetic information between wheat and other plants.

James Zahnley and Donald D. Kasarda also at the Food Proteins Unit at the ARS Western Regional Research Center are studying the characterization of molecules and mechanisms that affect formation of constituents in wheat grain.

Wheat storage protein biosynthesis takes place on the endoplasmic reticulum, an extensive membrane structure in developing endosperm cells. The scientists are working on the nature of the proteins of this membrane and the roles they play in translation of mRNA into storage protein.

Initial phases of the research have involved development of the methods for preparation of purified endoplasmic reticulum. Subsequently, proteins will be purified from the membrane and their reaction with polysomes and immature storage protein polypeptides (prepared by in-vitro translation of mRNA) will be investigated.

A project studying the molecular cloning of stress genes in cereal crops is being conducted at the ARS Western Regional Research Center in Albany California with lead scientist, William Hurkman. The scientists are studying the effects of environmental stresses, particularly those of salt water, and temperature on barley plants, and they intend to identify and characterize gene products and genes that are related to the response of barley to stress. They feel that the identification and isolation of genes that are exposed during stress will provide the capability to develop new genetic variants of cereal plants that are more tolerant to environmental stresses by genetic engineering techniques.

Researchers at the ARS Fruit and Vegetable Chemistry

Research Unit in Pasadena California report that there is promising research in the area of studying the <u>bioregulation of yield and quality of rubber in guayule.</u>

Henry Yokoyama reports that the single major obstacle to commercial production of natural rubber from the guayule plant is the low yield, and so far this has stimulated research towards increasing the rubber yield from this plant.

A promising approach to improving yield characteristics is through bioregulation of the synthesis of cis-polyisoprenes to cause an accumulation of increased amounts of rubber. This approach is based on the discovery of bioregulatory agents which stimulate the production of rubber in the guayule plant. So far, the most effective bioregulatory agent discovered is DCPTA, and it has been found in greenhouses and field studies that DCPTA causes up to two to three fold increase in the rubber yield from the guayule plant. Studies on the mode of action of DCPTA show the bioinduction of a multitude of enzymes and strongly suggests that regulation of gene expression is involved. These observations have important implications to improving agricultural crop productivity and quality by plant bioregulation.

Research on the <u>maturation and senescence of fruits, vegetables and seeds</u> is being conducted at the ARS Western Regional Research Center in Albany California with lead scientist J. Corse. Studies are directed towards the isolation and identification of the enzyme systems that control concentrations of cytokinins, gibberellins, indol-3-acetic acid and abscisic acid. The experiments are being done to determine exact hormonal concentrations during growth, flowering and senescence in small tissue samples and at the cellular level.

In another project at the ARS Western Regional Research Center, Sui-Sheng Hua is studying the <u>genetic regulation of symbiotic nitrogen fixation in the rhizobium-legume system and the mechanism of salt tolerance.</u> Nitrogen is a key limiting nutrient for plant productivity, and legumes such as soybean and alfalfa are capable of fixing nitrogen through Rhizobium-legume symbiosis. The rhizobia become associated with legumes by forming root nodules. Rhizobial genes defining nodulation and nitrogen fixation are induced or repressed in response to regulatory signals which act at specific stages of root nodule development. In field situations, soil nitrogen, salinity, temperature and microbial competition prevent the utilization of the full capacity of symbiotic nitrogen fixation.

Genetic improvement of this symbiosis is highly desirable to meet the demand of supplying sufficient fixed nitrogen for high yield of crops. In working on this project, the scientists have applied recombinant DNA technology, gene transfer, transposon mutagenesis and other biochemical and immunological methods to gain the basic knowledge of molecular mechanism of symbiotic nitrogen fixation and cellular adaptation to salinity stress.

A genomic library of salt tolerant rhizobium has been

constructed by cosmid cloning, and they are in the process of identifying and isolating genes which confer salt tolerance, identifying activator genes of ntirogen fixation in rhizobium, studying the root hair curling gene expression. The potential benefits of this research will be to increase crop productivity by maximizing nitrogen fixation and improving soil fertility for plant growth.

Researchers at the ARS Western Regional Research Center with lead scientist Thomas McKeon are working on the regulation and role of ribonuclease in plant development and senescence. The project is directed at showing how plants may control genetic expression. The scientists are studying the genetic regulation of ribonuclease during plant developmental processes because ribonuclease is a gene product which is differentially expressed during development, and it has the potential for mediating changes in genetic expression by altering ribonucleic (RNA) metabolism.

The researchers are characterizing two ribonucleases which have been isolated and purified from ripening tomato fruit. This characterization will allow the scientists to propose specific roles for the ribonucleases and the purified enzymes will then be used to provide the immuno-chemical probes for the next stage of work on messenger RNA isolation, characterization, and quantitation. Results suggest that ribonucleases do play a role in development and this research should contribute to the knowledge needed to insert well-regulated genes in plants.

Research is going on at the Nitrogen Fixation and Soybean Genetics Laboratory at the ARS Beltsville Agricultural Research Center in Beltsville Maryland to improve crops and plants. One project with lead scientist David Kuykendall is studying how to <u>engineer new Rhizobium gene combinations to improve biological nitrogen fixation abilities and subsequently legume crop yield and quality.</u>

Rhizobium bacteria change nitrogen from the air into a form that is used by plants and in this process Rhizobium live in nodules of the roots of legumes, and since both the bacteria and the host plant benefit from this intimate relationship, it is said to be "symbiotic". This symbiotic nitrogen fixation is controlled by genetic mechanisms. The goal of Rhizobium genetics research is to define these mechanisms and to manipulate them to produce improved and enhanced benefits to agronomic crop plants.

Plasmids are relatively small circles of DNA found in bacteria, and transposons are jumping genes that bacterial geneticists use as tools for marking and thereby identifying genes. Results of this research indicate that the plasmids of Rhizobium can be manipulated using transposons, and plasmid gene transfers are now possible with new gene combinations being made. The impact on science and agriculture will help to develop gene mapping systems and to construct genetically superior Rhizobium strains. The final result could mean marked increases in crop production through the use of genetically improved Rhizobium as inoculum for legumes.

At the Plant Hormone Laboratory at the ARS Beltsville Agricultural Research Center, Jerry Cohen is studying the regulation of plant hormones with a research project to specifically study the <u>regulation of the indole acetic acid level in plants</u> .

The rate of growth of plant cells which are capable of elongation is generally associated with the levels of the plant hormone indol-3-acetic acid (IAA). Exogenous application of IAA to growing tissues increases growth rates, causes acidification of cell walls, and induces ethylene biosynthesis. The plant tissue is also capable of metabolizing IAA quickly by adding either a sugar or an amino acid molecule to the active hormone. These conjugated IAA compounds are by themselves inactive, but if they are hydrolyzed they will yield free IAA.

Experiments are being done to determine if conjugation reactions and utilization of IAA-conjugates represent a mechanism by which cells regulate IAA levels. Tissue culture techniques are being used to monitor the biological activity of various conjugates as well as trying to produce various mutants. Information developed from such studies should help lead to a better understanding of how plant hormones are regulated in-vivo and lead to the development of new plant growth regulators and herbicides.

Another project underway at the Plant Hormone Laboratory at the ARS Beltsville Agricultural Research Center under the direction of James Anderson and James Baker is studying the regulation and control of ethylene biosynthesis and action. Most all crop plants synthesize and respond to the gaseous plant hormone ethylene. Generally, ethylene biosynthesis is associated with plant senescence and fruit ripening, but it is also important in breaking seed dormancy.

The biosynthetic pathway starting with the amino acid methionine has been elucidated and the regulated step (amino cyclopropane carboxylic acid synthesis) in the biosynthetic pathway has been determined. The researchers are attempting to isolate, purify and make antibodies to this rate limiting enzyme, and they are also attempting to clone the gene of this enzyme. They have partially purified a protein that induces ethylene biosynthesis very rapidly in some plant tissues, and they are studying how this protein applied to leaf tissues induces the cells in that tissue to activate the synthesis of ethylene.

The results indicate that ethylene induces new proteins to be synthesized as well as stopping the synthesis of other proteins. The scientists feel that understanding and being able to control ethylene synthesis and action should lead to techniques that will allow scientists to improve fruit quality and determine when various commodities should be marketed.

A research project under the direction of C.R. Caldwell at the Plant Stress Laboratory at the ARS Beltsville Agricultural Research Center is researching environmental factors with a specific project studying the physiology, biochemistry, and cytology of stress effects on plants. Alterations in the structure and function of plant plasma membranes induced by environmental factors could provide the trigger for plant adaptation to stress and the basis for stress induced damage.

Current research involves the in-vitro analysis of the effects of temperature and heavy metal cations in the dynamics of barley root plasma membranes. Fluorometry, electron paramagnetic resonance spectroscopy, and laser induced transient spectroscopy are being used to monitor the mobilities and interactions of plasma membrane proteins and lipids in an attempt to correlate alterations in membrane structure with changes in membrane bound enzyme activities.

At the Plant Genetics and Germplasm Institute at the ARS Beltsville Agricultural Research Center, the researchers are studying the genetic and developmental analyses of lectins during seed maturation and germination under the direction of Lila Vodkin.

Improving the quality and quantity of seed proteins in a major agronomic crop such as in soybeans is a long term objective. Using the techniques of molecular cloning and DNA sequencing, the gene which codes for a specific seed protein (soybean lectin) has been isolated and characterized, and this gene contains a signal sequence which directs the packaging of the lectin into the membrane bound protein bodies of the seed.

In an effort to determine the factors that regulate accumulation of seed proteins, scientists have determined the molecular basis for a genetic defect that prevents production of lectin protein in several soybean varieties. The basis for this mutation is the presence of a large segment of DNA which interrupts the lectin gene and prevents its expression. Sequencing studies have shown that this DNA segment has the structural features of a transposable element.

To date molecular analyses of mobile elements in plants has been obtained only for corn and a few other species. Mobile elements are capable of changing their positions in the chromosomes and they have utility as molecular tags for the purpose of physically isolating genes whose protein products are unknown. Many traits important to the plant breeder fall into this category.

Long range research will determine whether the soybean element can be used as a means to isolate soybean genes of agronomic importance or aid in the construction of transformation vectors for directed genetic engineering of plants. In addition, knowledge of the lectin gene structure will be utilized to assess whether soybean protein can be modified by reintroducing altered genes into the plants by genetic transformation methods.

At the ARS Southern Regional Research Center, scientists under the direction of Kenneth Ehrlich are working on a project that is studying the <u>conversion of soybean and cottonseed to meals</u>

with improved qualities through biotechnology techniques.

The basic objective of the program is to develop new approaches, using biotechnology which will improve the digestibility, palatability, and the safety of soybean and cottonseed meals.

To do this, researchers will use two different approaches using enzymes. One is to review undesirable metabolites by the treatment of the wetted meal with specific degradative enzymes, and the other is to blend acid-stable, specific degradative enzymes with meal prior to its use as a feed.

The required enzymes will be identified from microbial, plant, or animal sources. To increase enzyme availability, recombinant DNA methodology will be used in combination with classical mutagenesis and selection strategies. The researchers are looking for ways to control expression of in-situ plant genes involved in biosynthesis and degradation metabolites which affect soybean cottonseed quality.

In projected studies, the genes for fungal phytase will be isolated and cloned in E. coli and/or A. nidulans using cDNA cloning and genomic cloning. The cloned genomic DNA for phytase will be S1 mapped to determine whether insertion sequences are present and to locate transcription initiation or enhancer sequences for the gene. The gene will then be introduced into an appropriate bacterial species such as an amplifiable plasmid and this engineered species will then be used to generate large quantities of phytase. The scientists are also studying the factors which affect phytate formation and degradation in cottonseed or soybean plants.

Scientists at the ARS Horticultural Research Laboratory in Orlando Florida under the leadership of G. Yelenosky are working on a project that relates to citrus fruits, which is studying plants and their abilities to overcome cold weather conditions. Freeze damage in world agriculture is probably the major obstacle in world food production. Research of this type is expected to increase the fundamental understanding of plant function and bioregulation necessary to overcome freeze stress situations of short and long durations.

The objectives of the project are in finding the "triggering-controlling" mechanisms that will alleviate the problem without excessive expenditures in energy systems and help to establish data for freeze conditions in nuclear scenerios.

The researchers will use a variety of biotechnological tools that will interface with controlled environment facilties. These include the use of a)immunoelectrophoresis for specificity in micro-analyses of enzymatic reaction, protein synthesis, membrane-binding, conjugateal complexes, b) gene isolation-searches through natural selection with hopes to interface with protoplast-fusion technology, c) radioisotope markers for chasing synthesis and partitioning of metabolites, and d) chemical markers for identifying essential physiologically-sensitive sites vulnerable to artificial bioregulants.

Results of the research are expected to increase fundamental understanding of plant function and bioregulation to overcome freeze stress situations of short and long durations. The results will expedite technology transfer for immediate use in applied situations to prevent freeze damage, and to help control problems in world agriculture. This research will also produce scientific "know how" into the survival mechanisms that will be needed for nuclear scenarios.

At the Plant Science Research Unit in the Plant Pathology Department at the University of Florida, researchers are studying gene isolation, expression, and mapping in maize and sorghum under the direction of D.R. Pring and P.S. Chourey.

Three major problems are being studied and these include a) the isolation and characterization of genes conditioning cytoplasmic male sterility and maternal inheritance of disease susceptibility, b) the determination of regulatory modes for temporal and constitutive expression of genes associated with carbohydrate metabolism, and c) the development of protoplast culture methods for suitable application of vector DNA molecules.

The objectives are to isolate key genes, determine their mode of regulation, assemble appropriate regulation sequences, and vector these DNAs into recipient maize and sorghum tissue culture cells. Biotechnological tools being used include the cloning, via plasmid and cosmid vectors of key sequence from wild-type and mutant plants and tissue culture cells, and determining transcriptional activity, and sequencing of transcribed regions. Potential recombinant DNA vectors, including endogenous transposons and mitochondrial transposon-like molecules are being utilized for transposon mutagensis of coding genes. Protoplast and cell suspension systems are also being developed along with construction of several potential vectors.

Results to date include the demonstration of the molecular basis of reversion to male fertility in male sterile maize, the identification of genes coding for metabolic processes in developing endosperms, and the demonstration of genomic instability in tissue cultures. It is anticipated that this project will contribute to the basic knowledge of the control of important plant processes, that it will allow the design of critical vector sequences for transformation, and it will identify key sequences which condition agronomically important processes.

Scientists with ARS and the University of Missouri at Columbia Missouri are involved in several research projects that involve corn. For instance one project under the direction of Jack Beckett is studying the chromosome segments from tropical maize and how to insert the chromosomes into U.S. corn lines. The methods for chromosome engineering of segments are well developed, but so far have only been carried out for one gene segment in corn. The project is testing the inherited characteristics of insertion carrying materials, and how chromosome segments and groups of genes control vigor, efficiency, and growth and form of corn plants.

ARS and the University of Missouri at Columbia under the direction of Edward Coe are also studying the mutations in the DNA of the chloroplasts and mitochondria of corn. The green chloroplasts of higher plants and colorless mitochondria contain DNA of their own that determines some of the genetic functions required for their function. This DNA is also involved in the regulation and control of the interplay between the nuclear DNA and these organelles.

The project is defining mutations that occur in the organelles resulting in modifications of the plants. Some of these mutations are caused by nuclear genes and may involve inherited changes that are outside the DNA, and others possibly involve transposable elements.

Two nuclear gene-induced mutations that have altered growth patterns show by molecular-genetic analysis restriction, fragments of DNA changes in the DNA that are unstable in the mitochondria. Other mutations are being derived from other geneticists and are being analyzed for occurrence, effects, genetic locations, and for the study of the nucleus-organelle interactions and their potential manipulation by genetic engineering methods.

There is considerable research going on at the ARS Northern Regional Research Center in Peoria Illinois to study the

<u>biochemistry of plant cell wall modification by micro-organisms</u> under the direction of Michael Gould.

The polysaccharides and lignin present in plant cell walls comprise the largest single source of renewable biomass on the earth. In order to make efficient use of these raw materials for feed and fuel production, it is necessary to understand the underlying structural and mechanistic parameters that affect conversion of cell wall materials into useful products.

In nature these conversions are accomplished with high efficiency by a variety of micro-organisms primarily through extracellular processes that are regulated by otherwise dependent functions of the microbial cell membrane. The mechanisms and regulation of these microbial membrane functions are being investigated through the use of isolation, purification, and reconstitution techniques.

Because the presence of lignin represents a major obstacle preventing efficient utilization of plant cell wall polysaccharides, research efforts are concentrated on understanding the biochemistry and cellular physiology of lignin biodegration.

Membrane fractions rich in lignin degrading activity have now been isolated and are being studied to determine the molecular mechanism of lignin/membrane interactions and the regulation of these reactions by membrane properties. The ability to alter cell wall structure and composition by controlled biological means would constitute a major breakthrough in the efficiency with which lignocellulosic biomass can be used for feed and fuel production.

A new research project under the direction of G.C. Crawford at the Northern Regional Research Center in Peoria, Illinois is studying the biochemical control of protein and starch synthesis during seed development and plant senescence.

The objective of the research is to identify the biochemical and physiological processes and the regulatory mechanisms which control the metabolism of amino acids and sucrose within the developing corn embryo and endosperm. Two biotechnological tools will be applied in this research. Kernels will be cultured in-vitro on a nutrient media containing isotopically labeled sucrose and amino acids, and protoplasts will be isolated from developing seed and used to determine the transport mechanisms and metabolism of carbon and nitrogen substrates across the cell membrane. The scientists hope that this research will provide the basic information necessary for the successful genetic manipulation of protein and carbohydrate quality by recombinant DNA technology.

Lastly, a project at the Northern Regional Research Center in Peoria Illinois under the direction of Rodney J. Botheast is studying genetic engineering of rumen micro-organisms.

The nutritional dependence of ruminants on their micro-flora makes them especially suited for improvement through genetic manipulation of their bacteria, however, the genetics of rumen bacteria have not been studied and are essentially unknown. Criteria for development of genetically engineered rumen micro-organisms with a wide range of physiological and competitive traits require that the bacteria responsible for a given process be isolated and identified, the biochemistry of the process be analyzed in detail, the regulation and physiology of the process be studied, genetic control mechanisms be established, and then selective alteration of these mechanisms be made by transfer of genetic information. Successfully engineered organisms can then be used to control digestion of specific feedstuffs, to regulate specific fermentation products, and to control growth of specific bacterial species for improved rumen function. Success with any or all of these approaches may result in highly valuable breakthroughs to allow more efficient conversion of agricultural biomass and they may also increase the bioavailability of polysaccharides which would constitute a major contribution to the farmer and consumer.

The following is information available from the USDA Current Research Information System on some of the genetic engineering research projects being done at the Agricultural Research Service.

RESEARCH INFORMATION FROM CRIS

At the ARS Narcotics Substitution Research Unit in Salinas, California investigators E.J. Ryder, J.D. McCreight and L.L. Hoefert are working on <u>genetics and breeding of lettuce and other leafy vegetables.</u>

The objective of the project is to do genetic studies and develop lettuce cultivars and germplasm with uniform maturity, horticultural and nutritional quality, and additionally to study disease, insects, and stress resistance. The research project will also study the breeding potential of related composites, crucifers and other leafy vegetables, and lastly collect and maintain valuable germplasm.

The scientists have done tests on promising lines under field conditions. A gene for early flowering in crisphead lettuce, has been tested as a tool for reducing the time required to backcross favorable genes into adapted cultivars. They have also tested 116 lettuce plant introductions for salt tolerance, and several may be useful for development of salt tolerant lettuce.

At the College of Tropical Agriculture and Human Resources at the University of Hawaii in Honolulu Hawaii, investigators B.B. Bohlool and H.H.Keyser are doing a <u>genetic engineering approach to the improvement of rhizobium japonicum/soybean symbiosis.</u>

The objective is to genetically engineer fast-growing Rhizobium japonicum strains for soybean cultivars to improve efficiency of atmospheric nitrogen fixation and inoculant production.

Recently discovered fast growing soybean rhizobia were

compared with slow growing strains for biochemical differences and plasmid content. While the fast growers share symbiotic host specificity with the typical slow growers, they appear more closely related on a biochemical basis to other fast growing species of Rhizobium.

Several of the diagnostic tests indicated that the fast growers do not fit into the Bradyrhizobium genus of the slow growers. All ten of the fast growing isolates examined contained from one to four plasmid of >100 megadaltons. Results indicated that restriction endonuclease patterns of plasmids from three isolates were vastly different. Acridine orange was effective in producing mutants cured of the largest plasmid in one of the strains, and it was also found that these mutants lost the ability to form nodules on soybean and wild soybean genotypes. The new fast growing soybean rhizobia may provide a better genetic system for the study of the soybean symbiosis than the slow growing B. japonicum.

At the Plant Virology Laboratory at the Beltsville Agricultural Research Center in Beltsville Maryland, investigators R.L. Steere, T.O Diener, J.M Kaper are doing basic research on viruses, viroids, mycoplasmas, spiroplasmas, fastidious bacteria and mycorrhizae.

The objective of the research is to conduct in-depth studies of the morphology , biochemical composition, physical chemical and biological properties, and also to research diagnostic approaches, and host-pathogen-vector relationships.

These studies will be done for viruses, viroids, virusoids, prions, mycoplasmas, spiroplasmas, mycorrhizal fungi, phloem and xylem inhabiting procaryotes, and any other novel pathogens which might be discovered during the duration of the research project.

The scientists are using appropriate techniques such as purification procedures, biochemical and biophysical approaches, serology light and electron microscopy, biological symptomatology, assay procedures, radioactive studies and other biotechnology and genetic engineering procedures. New methods and equipment will be developed as necessary to advance these studies.

So far serum-free media for in-vitro culture of spiroplasmas has been improved, new strains of corn stunt spiroplasma were isolated, and transfection of spiroplasma cells with spiroplasmavirus DNA was achieved. Germination of surface sterilized spores of the mycorrhizal fungus Glomus epigoem was enhanced by several associated bacteria, and procedures were developed to produce high concentrations of spiroplasmavirus and to isolate and purify its DNA for transfection experiments.

At the Florist and Nursery Crops Laboratory at the Beltsville Agricultural Research Center, investigators R. Griesbach, T. Arisumi, and P. Semeniuk are studying the genetic modification of florist and nursery crops utilizing tissue culture and biotechnologies.

The scientists are conducting research on the application of molecular biology in plant improvement, developing new methodology in biotechnology for manipulating genetic material using both natural and induced genetic modification, and conducting genetic and biochemical studies on the stability and expression of the transferred foreign genetic information in mitotic generations.

In-vitro fertilization techniques are being applied to overcome either pre- or post- fertilization barriers through in-ovo fertilization and in ovule and embryo cultures. The alternative methods that are being used include somatic hybridization or protoplast fusion technology. Researchers are trying to increase fertility through utilization of anther culture, and they are also studying variability in tissue cultures and new drugs.

These studies on variability include researching somaclonal variations, and doing genetic and biochemical studies on these variant plants to determine how much of this variability results from true genetic changes rather than to the pattern of gene regulation. Finally, research is being done to determine the feasibility of modifying germplasm through chromosome-mediated transformation by physically transferring single chromosomes between cells.

At the Fruit Laboratory at the Beltsville Agricultural Research Center the investigator R.H. Zimmerman is working on research to develop tissue culture techiques applicable to fruit production.

The researchers are working to develop techniques for tissue culture propagation of cultivars of pome fruits and small fruits, and they are studying the possibility of using tissues cultures as a tool in breeding programs to aid in the development of new cultivars.

A greatly simplified technique for rooting apple cultivars in-vitro was developed with rooting for most cultivars better than or equal to more complex methods previously used. The method consisted of standing cuttings in a liquid medium containing only auzin and sugar for 4 to 7 days in the dark, and then transferring the cuttings to small performing peat plugs. It was found that rooting is more rapid and acclimatization of the rooted plants is easier than with those rooted in an agar medium.

Most of the rooted plants produced in these experiments were grown in the greenhouse and then in a field nursery. These trees are being distributed to state experiment stations for cooperative work to evaluate genetic stability and the field performance at different sites.

A replicated field trial of tissue cultured "Jonathan" was established to compare nursery and greenhouse grown trees for establishing orchards. Several additional cultivars were produced and planted in the preliminary trial orchard, and additional cultivars, particularly spur types, were established in culture. Results from a replicated field trial showed that tissue cultured trees continued to grow more vigorously than those budded on seedling MM106 or M26 rootstocks.

At the Insect Pathology Laboratory at the ARS Beltsville Agricultural Center, investigator T.B. Clark is studying arthropod viruses: characterization, genetics and replication in-vivo and in-vitro.

Researchers are trying to characterize viruses from insect pests and evaluate their potential for use in pest management. The scientists are also determining the biochemical processes of virus invasion, and studying the replication and virulence and the genetic factors controlling these processes.

Characterization is being done by a combination of light and electron microscope studies and by biochemical analysis of the structural components of the virus. Researchers will determine the genetic relatedness to other viral isolates from the same or similar insect species by restriction endonuclease analysis of the viral genome and by nucleic hybridization tests.

Genetic manipulation is being done by either classical methods of viral recombination or by isolating, cloning, and transferring specific genes using the methods of plasmid insertion, splicing and ligation for genetic engineering. They are also doing in-vitro studies that will involve development of new cell lines, and studies are being done to find out the effects of cell nutrition and metabolism of virus replication.

At the Vegetable Laboratory at the ARS Beltsville Agricultural Research Center, principal investigator K.L. Deahl is studying the nature and mechanisms of pest resistance in major vegetables.

The objective of this project is to develop new approaches and control measures that utilize defense mechanisms inherent in plants dependent on the elucidation of the molecular events determining pathogenesis and resistance. The focus of this project is to develop basic information about the nature and mechanisms of resistance to pathogens and insects of major vegetables.

They are doing basic studies on host pathogen/pest interrelationships to determine mechanisms of plant resistance. The researchers are utilizing tissue culture technology, membrane physiology, microbial genetics, and biochemistry. The best available technologies using gene manipulation and biochemical analysis are directed toward elucidation factors contributing to resistance, and also towards testing the potential contributions that protoplast manipulation and culture can make toward the development of disease resistant germplasm.

At the University of Maryland in College Park Maryland, investigator A. Collmer is studying the <u>control of plant disease through induction of resistance.</u>

Scientists feel that the ever increasing need to improve our ability to control plant disease with minimum economic and environmental costs necessitates the development of a new generation of control measures that operate by better utilizing defense mechanisms inherent in the plant, and that the development of these control measures depends in turn on a better understanding of the molecular events determining pathogenesis and resistance.

This project will focus on bacterial plant pathogens as both inducers of resistance and as challenge pathogens since bacteria have the facility to be genetically manipulated, and also because the blocking of the bacterially induced hypersensitive response in plants is an amenable indicator of an experimentally resistant state. The best available technologies of gene manipulation and chemical structural analysis are being directed towards an elucidation of the host and pathogen molecules that mediate induced resistance.

As the research progresses techniques were developed to start a histological study of the alfalfa system involving Colletotrichum trifolli. Fluorescent compounds were found to be associated with the development of resistance at very early stages, and an HPLC method was developed to separate and quantitate these compounds. The bacterial induced resistance system presently involves several pathogens and sparophytes on a limited number of host plants. Populations of bacteria containing antibiotic resistance markers are followed within the plant which has been pretreated in several ways, and various pathogen compounds and metabolic inhibitors are being tested as inducers to suggest which bacterial components or metabolic pathways are involved in induced resistance.

At the Plant Physiology and Chemistry Research Unit at ARS in Ithaca New York, investigator R.W. Zobel is studying the rhizobotanical factors in nutrient uptake and utilization by plants.

The objective of the project is to understand and control those rhizobotanical characteristics which affect and effect nutrient uptake and utilization. Soil parameters such as water, temperature, and gaseous atmosphere will be monitored to characterize their relationship to observed differences in root morphology. This information will be used to produce similar modifications in the laboratory and green house and to test the ability of more advantageous response.

Research determined that neither increased CO_2 or increased or lowered C_2H_4 levels conditioned regeneration in soybean callus cultures grown under normal environmental and nutrient conditions. Starch accumulation by callus had little effect on root initiation from the callus, and was modified by appropriate hormone treatments.

It was shown that nitrogen content of sunflower leaves is a primary determinant of photosynthesis activity in the leaves within a canopy. Neither potassium nor phosphorus content had a direct effect on photosynthesis, and the researchers feel that the transpiration stream through evapotranspiration and resultant accumulation of cytokinins in leaves is responsible for partitioning nitrogen to specific plant leaves and thereby controlling canopy photosynthesis. The researchers have also constructed soil probes which are microprocessor controlled and operate independently of human intervention, and they use thermal conductivity techniques to measure soil water matrix potential and soil temperature at several depths through the rhizosphere.

Sampling time for a probe with 8 sensors is under 1 minute, making it possible to do large field experiments to document the temporal spatial variability in moisture and the temperature in the rhizosphere. Researchers hope that coupling these techniques with standard micrometerological techniques will make possible a complete description of the plant environment.

At the Genetics and Cell Biology Laboratory at the University of Minnesota in St. Paul Minnesota, investigators F.A. Enfield and D.T. North are working on the genetic improvement of laboratory populations of cotton boll weevil.

The objective of this project is to improve laboratory populations of cotton boll weevils through genetic manipulation thus making it more suitable to be used in mass rearing and as a release strain in a sterile insect release control program.

The researchers are trying to determine the genetic basis for increased post irradiation survival and whether there are any additional genetic variances in the previously selected population. Two large replications have been completed and they have done an evaluation on the nature of gene action for these genes affecting 14 day post irradiation survival. The scientists have also determined that the data indicates that most of the response to selection for radiation resistance could be attributed to a small number of genes.

At the ARS Biological Control Of Weeds Research Unit at Madison Wisconsin, investigators L.E. Towill and J.P. Helgeson are studying <u>somatic cell procedures for exchanging genetic information among the tuber-bearing solanum species.</u>

The objective of the project is to develop single cell vehicles for improving tuber-bearing Solanum species via cell-cell fusions, by selecting somatic variants and incorporating specifically prepared DNA sequences.

The scientists are isolating protoplasts from solanum species with various useful genetic markers, developing procedures to optimize survival and differentiation, and determining the effects of external plant growth substances on internal phytohormone levels as a guide to effective differentiation regimes. They are developing procedures to optimize the frequency of cell-cell fusions and cell DNA vehicle fusions in order to insure survival and subsequent differentiation of the fusion products. Additionally they are determining genetic variations of the fusion products and lines from cultured cells.

So far the scientists have completed initial testing of somatic fusions between Solanum species. A total of 53 potential fusion products have been identified at the callus level and plants that differ phenotypically from either parent have been differentiated from these calli. Evaluation of these first possible fusion progeny has been initiated and they appear to have double the number of chromosomes that should result from somatic fusion and they also appear to be more vigorous than the original parents. Potential screening markers in various lines have been evaluated for expression at the plant and cell level, and both frost resistance and metibuzin resistance appear to be expressed.

At the Plant Pathology Department at North Dakota State University in Fargo North Dakota, investigator R.L Kiesling is studying the interaction of barley stripe mosaic virus and barley.

The goal of the project is to conduct research on the nature of differences among strains of the barley stripe mosaic virus (BSMV), and to study the nature of differences among eneotypes of barley and the effect on the interaction of this host pathogen system.

The genome of barley stripe mosaic virus was analyzed through the use of pseudorecombination techniques. Attempts were made to identify the RNA species responsible for seed transmissibility as well as for pathogenicity to oats and several barley cultivars, but the results of seed transmission experiments were unclear and required repetition. The activity of two isozyme systems, acid phosphatase and acetylesterase, were also studied in the BSMV resistant and suceptible barley cultivars, and the results indicated that acid phosphatase activity was significantly changed in both cultivars as a result of BSMV infection.

At the ARS Soil Plant Nitrogen Research Unit in Brookings South Dakota, investigators P.L. Guss, J.L Krysan and R.D. Gustin are studying the reproductive biology of corn rootworms.

The objective of the project is to determine the chemical basis for sexual communication among the Diabrotica species, the factors affecting ovipositional behavior of Diabrotica species in the field and laboratory, and the relationship between reproductive development and external and internal events during the life of the Diabrotica species.

The scientists are observing the effect of natural and related synthetic compounds on sexual behavior, and conducting controlled experiments under varied natural and laboratory conditions to establish environmental parameters influencing oviposition. They are also doing studies on the reproductive development as it relates to hormonal and biochemical reponses, nutrition, and mating and oviposition behavior.

At the Crops Pathology and Genetics Research Unit at the ARS Northern Regional Research Center in Peoria Illinois, investigators R.W. Detroy, N.J. Alexander and S.N. Freer are studying <u>molecular genetics technology for microbial production of plant polysaccharide-degrading enzymes</u>

The objective of the project is to determine and evaluate techniques in recombinant DNA technology for application to micro-organisms in order to increase the production of enzymes that degrade plant polysaccharides that are glycolytic.

The scientists are isolating and characterizing extrachromosomal DNA from fungi capable of being used as cloning vectors in DNA transformation. They are also investigating specific cloning techniques in the transformation of key polysaccharide degrading enzymes, cellulases, and amylases from one host to another, and studying cell fusion and cloning to enhance the synthesis of starch/cellulose saccharifying enzymes in bacteria/fungi. They are also studying fractionation of DNA fragments obtained from procaryotic/eucaryotic organisms prior to transformation work, and lastly, they are screening for enzymatic processes desired in recombinant cells using molecular genetics methodology.

At the ARS Citrus and Subtropical Products Laboratory in Gainesville Florida, investigator M.D. Huettel is studying the genetics of sterility in Heliothis.

The objective of the project is to compare the structure of the mitochondrial DNA in the various species of Heliothis. The researchers are also investigating the interactions between the nuclear and mitochondrial genomes during spermatogenesis, and the role of these interactions in inherited male sterility and whether this sterility can be induced by genetic engineering methods.

Scientists are using electrophoresis of the restriction enzyme digestion products of mitochondrial DNA to develop detailed comparative maps of the genomes of the various species and along with other methods to estimate H. Virescens hybrid ratios. Basic cytological, biochemical, and molecular genetic studies are being conducted on the role of the mitochondrion in spermatogenesis, and the genetics of mitochondrial membrane proteins are being investigated using the Heliothis hybrid system in order to identify aberrations in normal protein interactions. The molecular genetic basis of these aberrations will be elucidated and other methods for the induction of these aberrations in other species will also be investigated.

9

Information on Research Within the USDA Cooperative State Research Service

SPECIAL RESEARCH GRANTS AND THE COMPETITIVE RESEARCH GRANT PROGRAM

Biotechnology research within the USDA Cooperative State Research Service takes place within the Competitive Research Grants program and until recently in the Special Research Grants program. The Special Research Grants were eliminated in the 1986 budget but were previously awarded to land grant colleges, universities, research foundations established by land grant colleges and universities, state agricultural experiment stations, and to all colleges and universities who demonstrated a capacity to carry out research for the purpose of expanding promising and critical breakthroughs in the areas of food and agricultural sciences.

Some of the highlights of the Special Research Grants Program included:

--Research on dried beans was done to develop better varieties of dry edible beans and to evaluate and improve edible dry beans for disease resistance, nitrogen fixing efficiency, cold tolerance, protein quality, cooking quality and digestibility, and pod and seed dry matter accumulation.

--Research on blueberry shoestring virus control was conducted to try to broaden the blueberry germplasm base of sources for breeding improved varieties, and to discover cost effective insecticides for blueberry aphid control.

--Soybean research addressed the major problems of increasing productivity, nitrogen fixation, and reducing pest damage.

--Soybean Cyst Nematode research dealt with the search for new sources of nematode resistance and determination of the mechanism of inherited resistance. Because the soybean cyst nematode has the capacity to form many new races, work is also aimed at a better understanding of this pest's genetic diversity.

--Research on Tck Smut was done in a collaborative effort in the Pacific N.W. in collaboration with scientists at ARS. This research program has developed along several lines. Collections of wheat germplasm are being screened for new sources of Tck Smut resistance. Scientists are crossing wheat with other grass species, working on new chemical treatments for grains in market channels, screening fungicides as an additional strategy to control field infection, and improving methods for assessing TcK Smut disease crosses.

--Scientists developed new and better potato varieties in order to develop high yielding, and high quality varieties with better resistance to diseases, insects, and environmental stresses.

The Competitive Research Grants Program is relatively new having been established by the 1977 Farm Bill. Awards have been made in biological nitrogen fixation, biological stress on plants, genetic mechanisms for crop improvement, photosynthesis and human nutrition. The new biotechnology initiative within this program is going to study structure, functions, and organization of plant and animal genomes, transfer, expression, and regulation of genes and gene complexes, and gene-based control of growth, development and resistance to stress.

Approximately 857 research proposals were received for the biotechnology deadline of March 1, 1985 for the Competitive Research Grants Program. The proposals addressed the need to increase understanding of the structure, function, regulation and expression of genes and gene products. Other proposals would study the molecular basis of chromosome replication, interaction of chromosomal and extra chemosomal genes, how genes move about, and the basic mechanisms for interaction with beneficial or deleterious micro-organisms.

The second broad area addressed in the proposals deals with suboptimal growth in agriculturally important plants and animals. Proposals also want to research metabolic processes that influence growth and development. Additionally, proposals aimed to identify molecular, cellular or organismal targets for genetic manipulation.

The third category of proposed research relates to genetic and molecular mechanisms that control responses of the agricultural plant or animal to physical and biological stresses. Research goals on the plant, animal, or their associated microbes emphasize the identification, isolation, transfer, and expression of genes that are regulated by or involved in stress. Other proposals in this category would attempt to analyze genes that are likely to affect performance of the organisms under stress and to understand the molecular mechanisms underlying the organisms responses to stress. Other proposals aimed to understand the fundamental mechanisms of stress response, injury, tolerance and avoidance at the molecular, cellular, and organismal levels.

Highlights of recent progress in the grant program:

--Genetic engineering is used to reveal the properties of the photosynthetic system- Recombinant DNA techniques are being used by scientists at several institutions to investigate reactants in the photosynthetic system. These efforts serve to determine precisely which amino acids of a large enzyme protein molecule are active in its reactivity, which genes control the formation of the enzyme, particularly its active site, and how mutations can be used to produce enzymes of greater efficiency. At Michigan State University investigators have succeeded not only in cloning a gene for the enzyme active in carbon dioxide fixation, but also to have that gene expressed in the cloning vector. The next step will be to attempt to mutate the cloned gene.

Investigators at the University of Missouri are performing similar experiments in order to determine the characteristics of the oxygen evolving apparatus and the membrane in which it is imbedded. They have developed a cloning vector which itself is a photosynthetic organism. By the use of mutants, they will be able to learn which of the intermediates in oxygen evolution exert control over the transport of electrons through the system.

At Rockefeller University, scientists have isolated and sequenced the gene encoding the protein which binds to chlorophylls a and b. The chlorophyll a/b protein complex is the major light receptor of the leaf.The sequencing of the gene reveals the amino acid sequence of the protein, and thus it is now possible to examine its structural and catalytic characteristics, particularly its interaction with chlorophyll.

--Researching and increasing efficiency of nitrogen fixation through study of hydrogen cycling- Rhizobia are among the bacteria which when growing in symbiosis with certain legumes are capable of reducing molecular nitrogen to ammonia, a form of nitrogen that is utilized by plants. This reaction is catalyzed by the enzyme nitrogenase. There is an energy wasting side reaction associated with this enzyme in which hydrogen ions (H^+) are converted to hydrogen gas (H_2). Some rhizobia possess an enzyme hydrogenase that catalyzes the reoxidation of the hydrogen and the recovery of a significant percentage of the energy lost. Research groups at several laboratories have been investigating the mechanism of the latter reaction and have been trying to improve the efficiency of the recovery system by transferring the hydrogen recycling capacity to rhizobia that do not possess it.

Oregon State University has cloned the genes for hydrogenase from a strain of rhizobium japonicum, a bacterium that infects soybeans. They transferred these genes to a mutant that does not have the recycling capacity. Their goal is to transfer the genetic material to strains of rhizobia which do not possess significant hydrogenase activity such as those that infect alfalfa and clover.

At Johns Hopkins University, mutants of rhizobia with greater capacity for hydrogen uptake have been obtained. Biochemical characterization of various mutants is in progress to establish the mechanism of the hydrogenase system.

At the University of California, Davis, researchers are finding that the host has a significant effect on the extent of hydrogen evolution. They are finding that some genotypes of peas cause different levels of hydrogenase activity in the rhizobium.

A project just funded at the University of California at Riverside will involve study of the inhibition constant of hydrogen for inhibition on N_2 reduction by nitrogenase. Partitioning of electrons between N_2 and H^+ will be studied. These studies should lead to a clearer understanding of the mechanism by which energy is lost, and the development of ways to prevent or circumvent it.

--Studying the factor that determines the high efficiency of the primary photosynthetic reaction- In photosynthesis the primary light reaction is the excitation of a membrane imbedded pigment molecule. At Amherst College researchers are determining how this excited extremely reactive molecule is able to transfer an electron with high efficiency to an acceptor molecule nearby in the membrane, thus making light energy available for growth and crop production. From fast laser flashes, polarized light, and magnetic fields, researchers have determined that the distance and orientation of the acceptor molecule is the significant factor in preventing energy losses in wasteful back reactions. These findings will lead to a better understanding of how light energy is transformed into chemical energy.

COMPETITIVE RESEARCH GRANTS FROM THE CURRENT RESEARCH INFORMATION SYSTEM

The following selected information has been obtained from the USDA Current Research Information System on the Competitive Research Grants Program in the areas of genetic mechanisms, photosynthesis, gene identification, gene transfer, gene regulation, and nitrogen fixation.

RESEARCH ON GENETIC MECHANISMS

At the University of Wisconsin in Madison Wisconsin, investigators S.J. Peloquin and R.E. Hannemann are studying the use of meiotic mutants for the exploitation of solanum germplasm.

The objective of the research is to develop new high yielding cultivars through the use of Solanum species, haploids, and 2n gametes in order to broaden the genetic base of cultivated potatoes. The researchers will evaluate haploids for their ability to put wild species germplasm in a useable form, and they will determine the frequency and mechanism of 2n egg formation. They hope to develop a wide range of 2x haploids in regard to maturity, shape, dormancy, and disease resistance for use in 4x x 2x and 2x x 2x crosses.

The scientists are using four types of crosses to obtain new seedlings. Haploids of cultivars will be crossed to 16, 24-chromosome wild species to determine which haploids are most effective in giving F(1) hybrids with good tuber yield and type. Then the male fertility of the haploid-species F(1) hybrids will be evaluated to determine which species possess dominative genes which interact with the sensitive cytoplasm of Tuberosum to result in male sterility.

At Michigan State University in East Lansing Michigan, investigator G.L. Bush is studying the genetics of host selection in rhagoletis fruit flies.

The scientists are going to complete a phenotypic and genetic analysis of the host plant selection behavior and survival abilities of two species within an important group of fruit infesting flies within the genus Rhagoletis.

The research on these insects may serve as a model system for understanding the biological mechanisms involved in the formation of new races or biotypes of phytophagons insect pests.

The scientific experiments will analyze the host selection behaviors and survival abilities of R. mendax and R. pomonella and their hybrid progeny. This will be accomplished through detailed behavioral studies of preoviposition, oviposition, and postoviposition responses of the adult progeny to blueberry and apple host fruits and to surrogate agar fruits which are impregnated with chemicals existing on the surface of blueberry and apple fruits. The researchers will rear mendax, pomonella and their hybrid progeny in both blueberries and apples, and this will enable the scientists to complete a genetic analysis of the survival abilities of mendax and pomonella in both host fruits.

At North Dakota State University in Fargo North Dakota, investigator N.D. Williams is studying induced mutations of sporophytic and nucleo-cytoplasmic sterility mechanisms in common wheat.

The objective of the research is to obtain mutations of the cytoplasmic or nuclear genes controlling sporophytic and cytoplasmic sterility mechanisms, and to study the fertility restoration systems in wheat.

They will use mutagenic chemicals to treat the seeds of wheat, which will induce genetic changes. They will then examine progenies for maternally inherited cytoplasmic sterility, partial or complete female fertility and seed set in order to identify mutations affecting sporophytic or cytoplasmic male sterility.

At Texas A&M University in College Station Texas, investigor R.H. Smith is studying the <u>cellular selection of genetic variants in sorghum for breeding improvement.</u>

The researchers will select cellular level tolerance to aluminum, sodium chloride, and polyethylene glycol in sorghum callus cultures, and regenerate plants from callus on both short and long term selection. They will screen progeny of in-vitro derived plants for tolerance at the whole plant level to aluminum and sodium chloride. The researchers will also establish a correlation between the cellular-level mechanism for osmotic stress and whole plant responses, and identify and characterize the physiological parameters of osmotic selected callus and compare them to whole plants growing at a similar osmotic stress.

The researchers have initiated callus cultures from a regenerative sorghum variety. Plants are being generated and grown to maturity in the greenhouse and F(1) seed is being collected. The scientists will then collect physiological data on the callus cultures using HPLC and GC.

At Kansas State University in Manhattan Kansas, investigator A.K. Chatterjee is studying <u>genetics and expression of bacterial determinants of soft-rot diseases.</u>

The long term goals of this research is to clarify the genetic and physiological aspects of production of the pectolytic and pectinolytic enzymes in soft-rot bacteria and to elucidate the role of these enzymes in bacterial plant pathogenicity.

The immediate goal of this project is to develop the erwinia carotovora subsp. carotovora (Ecc) genetic tools required in the analysis of plant virulence genes, to elucidate the organization and expression of the genes that specify recombination proficiency and to study the production of extracellular polygalacturonase (PG) and to investigate the roles of PG and pectate lyase in plant pathogenicity of Ecc.

At Oregon State University in Corvallis Oregon, investigators D.W. Mok and M.C. Mok are working on the genetic regulation of cytokinin metabolism in food legumes.

The objective of the project is to characterize the genetics and biochemical mechanisms controlling the metabolism of the plant hormone cytokinin in beans (phaseolus species).

The researchers will identify genotypic variations in cytokinin metabolism in cell cultures and whole plant tissues. The genetic and biochemical mechanisms involved will be elucidated by progeny studies in conjunction with analyses of radioactively labeled cytokinin metabolites. The enzymes regulating cytokinin metabolism and their sub-cellular localization will be characterized, and at the same time the scientists will study the metabolism and mode of action of a highly active phenylurea-type cytokinin, (Thidiazuron).

Also at Oregon State University in Corvallis Oregon, investigators D.J. Armstrong and T.C. Moore are studying the genetic regulation of hormonal metabolism in food legumes.

The objective of the project is to identify genetic factors and regulatory mechanisms that control hormonal metabolism in the food legumes (Phaseolus and related genera.)

Scientists have identified interspecific and intraspecific variations in cytokinin metabolism present in tissue cultures of Phaseolus genotypes, and these will be characterized by biochemical and genetic analysis. Genetic variations being studied include the expression of cytolinin autonomy, responses to cytokinin active areas, and the differential metabolism of cytokinin with unsaturated N -side chain.

At the University of California at Davis California, investigator C.I. Kado is doing a molecular analysis of the virulence region of the agrobacterium plasmid PTIC58

Scientists know that attempts to improve crop plants by the use of genetic engineering technology have been limited by the lack of a suitable plant cloning vector. Current research is directed towards the development of such a vector from the large Ti plasmids present in tumor-inducing strains of A. tumefaciens. Results indicate that while the region of DNA that is incorporated in the plant genome (T-DNA) may play a crucial role in the development of a vector, a second region of the plasmid, the virulence region is involved in the transfer of DNA from the bacterium to the plant. An understanding of the function of the virulence region may be crucial to the use of plant cloning vectors.

This project involves determination of the nucleotide sequence of critical sectors of the virulence region. E. coli minicells, maxicells and a cell-free A. tumefaciens coupled transcription-translation system are used to locate genes encoding polypeptide products within these sectors. Regulatory regions (promoters) are identified by the formation of filter retainable complexes of DNA with purified A. tumefaciens RNA polymerase, polymerase protection studies, and high resolution S1 nuclease mapping. The results obtained in this study should help establish the molecular genetics of the virulence region and the regulatory mechanisms involved in the expression of virulence genes.

At the University of Washington in Seattle Washington, investigator W. Halperin is doing molecular and genetic studies of agrobacterium tumefaciens attachment mutants.

This project is studying the attachment of the plant pathogen Agrobacterium tumefaciens to plant cells. Goals include estimating the number and organization of chromosomal and plasmid encoded genes involved in attachment, identifying the bacterial cell surface properties determined by these genes, and using bacteriophages to study altered cell surface properties of attachment mutants.

Agrobacterium tumefaciens causes crown gall tumors on

dicotyledonous plants, and the mechanism of tumor formation includes transfer of bacterial Ti-plasmid DNA to plant cells where it is integrated into plant nuclear DNA.

An initial step in this pathogenic process is the attachment of Agrobacterium to plant cells. Such cell-cell interaction is important in the establishment of pathogenic intersections by many plant pathogens. The scientists have been studying the attachment process of Agrobacterium in hopes of identifying the genetic and biochemical basis for this ability, and they have identified several avirulent Agrobacterium mutants which contain transposon Tn5 in chromosomal DNA, and show defective attachment of plant cells. Genetic linkage between the Tn5 insertions and the avirulent attachment defective phenotype was demonstrated, indicating that the genes inactivated by these Tn5 insertions code for products necessary for attachment. Recombinant DNA techniques were used to construct clones of Tn5 containing DNA from the mutants, and analysis showed that all the insertions are clustered on a small region of the chromosome. This indicates that a small number of genes are involved, and that further analysis of this region needs to be studied.

At Washington State University in Pullman Washington, investigator A. Kleinhofs is studying the genetics of nitrate reduction in barley.

The long term goal is to understand the genetic regulation of nitrate assimilation in crop plants. Such knowledge is essential for the eventual genetic engineering of crop plants for improved nitrogen use efficiency. The scientists are conducting an intensive search for new genes controlling nitrate reductase activity, in order to study in detail the function of these genes. These studies should provide new insight into the genetic control and biochemical mechanisms of nitrate assimilation.

RESEARCH ON PHOTOSYNTHESIS

At the University of Maryland in College Park Maryland, investigator I.N. Foresth is studying the integration of leaf orientation and photosynthesis in response to environmental drought.

The objective of the project is to examine the role of rapid leaf movements in an agronomic setting in terms of cultivar differences, to study their effects on canopy light penetration, and study their integration with photosynthesis in responding to environmental drought. The researchers want to gain an understanding of how plants balance "behavior" and physiology to operate most efficiently under stress and non-stress conditions.

The scientists are examining whole leaf gas exchange responses to light, CO_2, and leaf water potential, and they are comparing the gas exchange responses of naturally and horizontally oriented leaves. They will combine these concrete measurements to provide an integrated picture of the stomatal, photosynthetic and morphological responses of plants to atmospheric and soil water stress.

At the University of Massachusetts in Amherst Massachusetts, investigator R.E. Blakenship is studying the mechanism of primary and secondary reaction in photosynthetic bacteria.

The project is using primary and secondary electron transfer reactions in photosynthetic bacteria, and the goal is to improve understanding of the mechanisms of the charge separation and stabilization.

At the University of Missouri at Columbia Missouri, investigator D. Miles is studying nuclear genes in corn which regulate proteins for chloroplast membranes.

The goal of the project is to better understand nuclear gene regulation of chloroplast development and of photosynthesis. Chloroplast genes for photosynthetic proteins are being rapidly described, however, there are few examples of nuclear genes regulating specific chloroplast proteins. The scientists are going to examine nuclear regulation by describing nuclear genes which encode protein components of the chloroplast membranes.

The researchers will induce photosynthesis mutants in maize with the transporable DNA element, mutator Mu1, and these mutants will be characterized to the specific reaction of photosynthesis. At this time restriction fragments of nuclear DNA containing Mu1 will be isolated and correlated with the mutant phenotype, and these will be cloned using standard methods of molecular cloning. The wild-type gene sequence will be recovered from a genomic library and/or the normal transcript will be isolated by hybrid selection. The protein products of these gene clones can then be characterized and correlated with similar well characterized mutations in maize, and cloned verified nuclear photosynthesis genes can then be sequenced.

Also at the University of Missouri in Columbia Missouri, investigator L.A. Sherman is studying <u>gene organization and cloning of photosynthesis genes in anacystis nidulans R2.</u>

The researchers are analyzing the organization of genes in cyanobacteria to determine if any photosynthesis genes are plasmid encoded isolating herbicide resistant and metal resistant mutants, and studying the use of such mutants for cloning of the appropriate genes. They are also cloning genes that code for Photosystem II proteins and manipulating these genes in-vivo and the gene products in-vitro in order to study the genetic and biochemical control of photosynthesis.

At the University of Nevada in Reno Nevada, investigator C.B. Osmond is studying <u>nitrogen use efficency in photosynthesis and responses to irradiance and water stress.</u>

The overall objective of this research is to provide an explanation in biochemical terms of nitrogen use efficiency in photosynthesis and the ways that it limits leaf photosynthesis in marginal agricultural environments characterized by limiting nutrients, water stress and high irradiance.

The scientists are growing spinach, sunflowers, and desert

annuals that are found in high and low nitrogen habitats. They are growing them at different nitrogen nutrient levels, and irrigating them under high and low irradiance. Leaf photosynthetic responses to intercellular CO_2 and irradiance will be analyzed in terms of recent hypotheses which describe the rate limitations of photosynthesis in terms of component biochemical processes.

At Oklahoma State University in Stillwater Oklahoma, investigator R.C. Johnson is studying the <u>stomatal behavior and photosynthesis in wheat under drought and at elevated CO_2.</u>

The objective of the project is to determine the relative contribution to reduced photosynthesis by stomatal behavior as compared with non-stomatal factors in wheat genotypes under different levels of drought stress. The researchers will determine how growth, photosynthesis, and water use efficiency are affected by elevated atmospheric CO_2 concentrations under drought in modern hexaploid wheats and wild wheat relatives.

The researchers will use growth chambers to grow plants at different ambient CO_2 concentrations and drought conditions. Photosynthesis, water use efficiency, and stomatal behavior will be studied using a steady state gas exchange measurement system.

At Purdue University in West Lafayette Indiana, investigator R.A. Dilley is studying the <u>chloroplast membrane-proton interactions related to photophosphorylations.</u>

The objective of the project to study how photosynthetic organelles, choloroplasts of higher plants convert energy from the primary oxidation reduction reactions into proton gradients and then into ATP.

At Cornell University in Ithaca New York, investigator R.M Spanswick is studying the role of membrane transport systems in the partitioning of photosynthate.

The objective of the project is to understand how the partitioning of photosynthetic and nitrogenous assimilates is controlled particularly in developing soybean seeds. The immediate goals are to investigate the relationship between partitioning and the membrane transport processes occurring in the seed coat, to develop cotyledons to construct a theoretical description of partitioning, and to test the resulting model.

Also at Cornell University in Ithaca New York, investigator R.E. McCarty is studying the transport of glycolic acid in photorespiration.

Photorespiration which is light dependent upon O_2 and the release of CO_2 limits photosynthetic yields. It is also known that transport of metabolites across the limiting membranes of chloroplasts, peroxisomes, and mitochondria is an essential part of photorespiration. The researchers want to transport glycolate, the substrate of photorespiration, across the envelope membranes of chloroplasts. Recent evidence suggests that glycolate uptake by intact chloroplasts is mediated with short times of incubation, and is inhibited by N-ethylmaleimide, by glyoxylate and glycerate.

At the University of California in Berkeley California,

investigator J.E. Hearst is studying <u>suicide quinones for photosynthesis.</u>

The principal objective of the project is to develop a reliable method for identifying quinone bending sites in photosynthetic membranes in order to sequence resolution in the appropriate protein structure. The researchers are synthesizing and testing suicide quinones that are designed to alkylate their binding sites when they are reduced by the natural electron transport process.

At the University of Florida in Gainesville Florida, investigator C.R. Johnson is studying <u>photosynthate partitioning in a mycorrhizal symbiosis</u>

The researchers want to clarify the basis for altered photosynthesis in mycorrhizal plants, and to identify and quantify factors regulating amounts of carbon allocated to the mycorrhizal fungal symbiont.

The scientists will split root citrus seedling for quantifying the amount of carbon allocated to the mycorrhizal symbiont. They will also study the photosynthate cost to the host plant for a mycorrhizal symbiosis by stimulating fungal sporulation utilizing plants of varying degrees of mycorrhizal dependancy, and by imposing varying degrees of osmotic stress to the host plant. Measurements will be taken on photosynthesis, respiration of tops and roots, and partitioning of photosynthesis following CO_2 exposure of tops.

Also at the University of Florida in Gainesville Florida, investigator K.E. Koch is studying <u>phloem unloading and photosynthate transfer in citrus fruits.</u>

Researchers are studying the path of photosynthate movement by combining autoradiographic data and previously completed studies of C assimilate transfer, by examining phloem unloading and transport through non vascular zones, and studying the enzymes and metabolic changes in photosynthates.

At the University of Illinois in Urbana Illinois, investigator C.A. Wraight is studying the <u>herbicide action and selectivity in photosynthetic electron transport.</u>

The scientists know that certain herbicides act to block electron flow through the acceptor quinone complex reaction centers from purple photosynthetic bacteria and the Photosystem II of plants. The scientists have proposed that the inhibition is a consequence of competitive displacement of quinone from the reaction center. They are using both bacterial and plant systems to study the kinetic and thermodynamic parameters of the inhibition and the structural basis for inhibitor binding and selectivity.

At the University of Illinois in Urbana Illinois, investigators A.R. Crofts and H.H. Robinson are studying the <u>mechanism of the reduction of plastoquinone by Photosystem II in chloroplasts.</u>

The objective of this research is to determine the binding constants and exchange rates of plastoquinone, plastoquinol, and plastosemiquinone at the Q(B) site, secondly, to understand the mechanism of the interference in the reduction of plastoquinone at the Q(B) site by photosynthetic herbicides, and thirdly to determine the kinetics of the oxidation reduction and protonation reactions involved in the reduction of plastoquinone at the Q(B) site of photosystem II.

Also at the University of Illinois in Urbana Illinois, investigator D.R. Ort is studying the <u>physiological and biochemical basis for chilling-impairment of photosynthesis.</u>

This research will establish exactly what chloroplast functions are disrupted by chilling and to discover the physical basis for the disruption. This should also uncover the essential differences which allow photosynthesis to continue after a chilling night in tolerant plants but not to continue in chill sensitive plants.

Photophosphorylation is among the most liable of chloroplast activities and it's a good candidate for disruption by unfavorable environmental conditions such as prechilling. In this study the researchers are doing experiments designed to study the possible effects of chilling on photophosphorylation and the various parameters critical to energy conservation. Presently they do not know if chilled induced malfunctions of one or more of the Calvin cycle enzymes might be an element for this disruption of chilling on photophosphorylation.

At Massachusetts Institute of Technology, in Cambridge

Massachusetts, investigator L.A. Steiner is studying reaction center protein in primary process of photosynthesis.

The objective of the project is to isolate and sequence analysis of peptides derived from the H subunit of reaction centers from the photosynthetic bacterium (Rhodopseudomonas spheroides) and to determine the carboxy-terminal sequence of the subunit.

The H subunit will be digested with trypsin and the resulting peptides fractionated by high pressure liquid chromatography. The amino sequence of the purified peptides will be determined by either automated Edman degradation or a manual dansyl-Edman procedure. The researchers will then use the data to collaborate results obtained by DNA sequence analysis of the gene encoding the H subunit.

At the University of Tennessee in Oak Ridge Tennessee, investigator F.C. Hartman is studying the characterization of phosphoribulokinase-a regulatory enzyme in photosynthesis.

As a regulatory enzyme in the Calvin cycle, phosphoribulokinase (PRK) improves the efficiency of CO_2 assimilation. The researchers are doing experiments designed to provide specific chemical information about the enzyme's active site, studying general structural information required for elucidation of the mechanism, and studying the relationship between the two forms of PRK.

At the University of Arizona in Tucson Arizona, investigator R.G. Jensen is studying the regulation of photosynthetic CO_2 assimilation in wheat and other plants.

This project hopes to provide understanding on how activation of the ribulose bisphosphate carboxylase regulates CO_2 assimilation in intact plant. The capacity of the wheat photosynthetic system to produce ribulose bisphosphate will be determined by extrapolative methods under various irradiances and CO_2 and O_2 levels. This will then be compared to the amount of activated carboxylase and apparent CO_2 exchange rates of intact wheat and other plants and this should help predict the conditions that limit photosynthesis either by active carboxylase or regeneration of the substrate ribulose bisphosphate.

RESEARCH ON GENE IDENTIFICATION, TRANSFER, AND REGULATION

At the University of Wisconsin in Madison Wisconsin, investigator E.T. Bingham is studying the alfalfa variants regenerated from cell cultures-genetic analysis of transfer to Breeding L.

The first objective of the project is to backcross two of the most interesting and potentially useful variant traits into elite northern adapted breeding lines, and secondly to use the best dominant and recessive traits identified to do more study and research in this area.

The two traits being studied include extra leafiness, and the other trait is a semidwarf which is also leafy and high in protein and low in fiber. Both traits behave as dominants and will be backcrossed twice into a Wisconsin Experimental possessing multiple pest resistance. The researchers feel that this could well be the first such releases in a field crop and would satisfy a long range project goal.

The scientists also hope to find out how much variation can be obtained from a single genome by cell culture, and they will investigate this by reculturing some of the existing fertile variants. They hope to find out if any variants revert to the donor phenotype when they are recultured and regenerated. A gene expression change in alfalfa tissue culture has been confirmed, and they are studying expression changes in other culture derived traits.

At the University of California in Davis California, investigator J. Dvorak is studying the transfer of quantitative traits-elytrigia salt tolerance to wheat by chromosome engineering.

The scientists will recombine wheat chromosomes with the chromosomes of Elytrigia elongata and E. pontica that control high tolerance to salinity, and they hope that these recombined chromosomes will ultimately be used to develop salt-tolerant wheat.

At Oregon State University in Corvallis Oregon, investigator R.S. Quatrano is studying control of gene expression during maturation of the wheat grain.

The scientists hope to understand the molecular and

physiological controls operative in the expression of embryo-specific gene sets during wheat grain development. This will involve the characterization of the embryo storage proteins, which will add to information concerning the homology of these proteins.

At the University of California in Berkeley California, investigator B.J. Staskawicz is doing a <u>molecular analysis of avirulence genes in pseudomonas syringae pv. glycinea.</u>

The researchers are studying the regulation and expression of the race 6 avirulence gene in E. coli maxicells. Northern blots will also be performed to determine the transcriptional regulation of this gene. The scientists will then identify avirulence genes by mobilizing individual clones into a compatible race of p.s. glycinea and then they will innoculate soybean plants.

At the University of Kentucky in Lexington Kentucky, investigator, R.J.Shepherd is <u>defining and mapping the genes of cauliflower mosaic virus.</u>

The researchers are studying the function, concentration, and distribution of the gene VI product of the cauliflower mosaic virus in infected plants since gene VI appears to be important in disease induction. Both conventional and molecular biological methods, particularly recombinant DNA techniques are being used to study the genetic constitution and disease induction by the caulimoviruses.

At the University of Missouri in Columbia Missouri,

investigator M.G. Neuffer is studying the <u>selection,</u>
<u>characterization and preservation of mutants in corn.</u>

The researchers are going to prepare and maintain a large
collection of chemically induced mutants in an easily accessible
form for agronomic and basic biological research. To obtain this
collection, the researchers will select desirable mutants by
developing special screening methods, so that they can preserve
large numbers of mutants already identified. The scientists will
classify, catalogue, and establish them in a vigorous uniform
background.

Also at the University of Missouri in Columbia Missouri,
investigator J.C. Polacco is studying <u>genetic regulation of a</u>
<u>seed-specific protein in soybean.</u>

The researchers are going to recover a soybean seed urease
cDNA clone and use it to determine the amount and specificity of
urease transcript in cotyledons, in the leaves and suspension
cultures of normal and urease negative soybeans. In this research,
they will explore genetic nutritional and environmental influences
on urease synthesis.

At Florida State University in Tallahassee Florida,
investigator M.Y. Menzel is studying the <u>development of a</u>
<u>cytogenetic manipulation system for cotton.</u>

The researchers want to develop a system of deficiency
and duplication chromosome markers for cotton and to identify
marker genes for as many of these chromosomes as possible, with

special emphasis on chromosomes 8, 11, 13, 14, 19, 21, 23, and 24.

At Purdue University in West Lafayette Indiana, investigator K.M. Herrmann is studying the regulatory mechanisms in the biosynthesis of aromatic compounds in higher plants.

The long term goal of this project is to identify specific DNA sequences that function as control elements in the expression of genes. The primary focus is on the DNA region(s) preceding the coding sequence(s) for 3-deoxy-D-arabino-heptulosonate 7-phosphate (DAHP) synthase from carrot (Daucus carota).

At Montana State University in Bozeman Montana, investigators, T.K. Blake and E.A. Hockett are studying the use of single copy cloned DNA sequences as a basis for gene mapping in barley.

The researchers are going to obtain cDNA derived probes from barley or related angiosperms and use these to identify restriction fragment length polymorphisms in different barley genotypes. They will then develop these and other genomic single copy DNA derived probes using the blotting methodology of Southern (1975) to a point at which useful recombination analyses may be performed. The goal is to cover the barley genome with at least 100 probes which identify restriction fragment length polymorphisms within commonly used genotypes of H. vulgare.

At the University of Georgia in Athens Georgia, investigator G.A. Galau is studying genetics and molecular biology of cotton cytoplasmic male sterility.

The researchers are studying the genetic and molecular basis of an alloplasmic-genetic male sterility which resulted when the Gossypium hirsutum nuclear genome was transferred into G. harknessii cytoplasm. The scientists feel that restoration of fertility is dependent on maintenance of a restorer gene (Rf) presumed to derive from G. harknessii. In their research they are creating via semigamy-mediated transfers, reciprocal combinations of cytoplasm and nuclear genomes of these species. They are examining leaves and anthers for alterations in gene structure or expression which correlates with phenotype. Analysis will be by restriction enzymes, in-vivo, in organello and in-vitro protein synthesis.

At the University of Notre Dame in Notre Dame Indiana, investigato M.J.Fraser Jr. is studying <u>the isolation of host range and temperature resistance genes of nuclear polyhedrosis viruses.</u>

The project is going to isolate a mutant gene from a nuclear polyhedrosis virus that confers resistance to inactivation by 35C. They will do this by transfer of the mutant gene to a cloned wild type virus, and they are also going to attempt to isolate regions of the viral genome which determines the host range of nuclear polyhedrosis viruses. The researchers are going to use gene transfer methodology, and transfer parts of a mutant viral genome to a wild type virus in-vitro.

At Texas A&M University in College Station Texas, investigator T.L.Thomas is studying <u>isolation of hormone regulated</u>

genes expressed during carrot somatic embryogenesis.

The objective of this project is to identify and isolate genes that are expressed during carrot somatic embryogenesis, and this should yield genes that are required for the normal ontogeny of the embryo as well as genes that are under tight phytohormone control.

RESEARCH ON NITROGEN FIXATION

At the University of California in Davis California, investigator D.N. Munns is studying the failure of phaseolus vulgaris to sustain N_2 fixation in the field.

The long term goal is to have successful bean production without nitrogen fertilizers. This research is going to select genotypes for their ability to meet their growth potential using biological nitrogen fixation combined with tolerance to common stresses in the field.

The researchers are testing host strain combinations claimed to be vigorous nitrogen fixers against nitrogen fertilized controls and successful soybean and cowpea symbioses. This symbiosis is compared at nodulation, middle stage, and pod filling, since different factors influence fixation at the different stages.

Also at the University of California in Davis California, investigator J.L. Ingraham is studying the physiological genetics of denitrification-a route to conserving fixed nitrogen.

The researchers are studying the process of biological denitrification emphasizing clarification of the metabolic intermediates of the pathway, the proteins that mediate the component reactions, and the regulation of expression of the genes encoding these proteins.

The scientists will emphasize the physiological genetic techniques of mutant isolation and analysis, using primarily the active denitrifying bacterium Pseudomonas stuzeri. They will also use standard biochemical techniques of protein purification, enzyme assay, gas chromatography, and high pressure liquid chromatography.

At Oregon State University in Corvallis Oregon, investigators D.E. Hibbs and S.R. Raddosevich are studying intra-specific and inter-specific interactions between red alder and douglas fir.

The researchers are measuring the effect of intraspecific and interspecific interactions in red alder in terms of individual plant response (growth rate, form, physiological parameters, and unit area productivity). They are doing this study at three sites in Washington and Oregon spanning a range of site fertility. At each site there will be alder density studies and alder Douglas fir replacement series. The scientists are measuring production, biomass allocation, leaf distribution, light extinction, nitrogen fixation, and soil moisture.

At Washington University in St. Louis Missouri, investigator K.R. Schubert is studying the intracellular organization of ureide synthesis in soybean nodules.

The researchers want to examine the intracellular organization of reactions associated with the assimilation of NH_4^+ and the synthesis of the ureides, allantoin and allantoic acid in soybean nodules. The scientists are using an experimental approach that involves subcellular fractionation, and subsequent biochemical and tracer studies with isolated organelles.

At Johns Hopkins University in Baltimore Maryland, investigator R.J. Maier is studying the <u>characterization of the hydrogen oxidation system in Rhizobium Japonicum.</u>

Bacteria of the genus Rhizobium infect the roots of legumes to form root nodules that allow the fixation of atmospheric nitrogen into a form utilized by the legume. One Rhizobium factor that increases N_2 fixation by soybeans occurs when the strain posseses an H_2 uptake system. This H_2 uptake system recycles the H_2 evolved by nitrogenase and returns the energy obtained from H_2 oxidation back into the nodule. The researchers are trying to understand the regulatory mechanisms acting on this H_2 uptake system and to identify the number and nature of the components involved in H_2 uptake.

At the University of Missouri in Columbia Missouri, investigator D.W. Emerich is studying <u>nitrogen fixation-energy generation via hydroxybutyrate and organic acid metabolism.</u>

The researchers are completing the characterization of Ketothiolase (KT). KT is characterized with regard to possible metabolic effectors. Glucose, acetate, NAD, and ATP will be added to the purified enzyme to find stimulation/inhibition. They are completing purification of hydroxybutyrate dehydrogenase (HBD). HBD is purified by typical methods and its physical chemical properties determined. The researchers are also characterizing HBD-deficient mutants. These mutants are being characterized in terms of various metabolic activities, polymer accumulation, nodule structure, and nitrogen fixation. Lastly, the researchers are isolating malate utilization mutants. These mutants will be selected after Tn5 mutagens by their inability to grow on malate.

At the University of Wisconsin in Madison Wisconsin, investigator J.C. Ensign is studying the role of vesicle organelle in nitrogen fixation in the actinorhizal bacterium Frankia.

The researchers are defining the properties of the specialized organelle of nitrogen fixation in the actinorhizal bacterium Frankia with work focusing on the mechanism of oxygen exclusion and the biochemistry of nitrogen fixation.

The organelles formed at the time when the organisms grow on atmospheric nitrogen will be isolated using physical means to disrupt cells followed by density gradient centrifugation. The scientists are studying chemical composition, enzyme complement, requirements for N_2 fixation, and then they are comparing the physiological studies of the respiratory rate and enzymes involved in electron transport with the mycelial cells grown in fixed nitrogen.

Appendix A

Information Sources

A

AGENCY FOR INTERNATIONAL DEVELOPMENT

320 21st Street N.W.

Washington, D.C. 20523

Telephone: (202) 632-1850

Description: Provides expertise and "know how" to foreign

governments in the scientific and technical fields.

AGRICULTURAL RESEARCH INSTITUTE

9650 Rockville Pike

Bethesda, Maryland 20814

Telephone: (301) 530-7122

Description: Studies problems and does research in agriculture.

Publishes a newsletter on a quarterly basis.

AMERICAN ASSOCIATION FOR THE ADVANCEMENT OF SCIENCES

1515 Massachusettes Avenue N.W.

Washington, D.C. 20005

Telephone: (202) 467-4400

Description: AAAS is an association for the sciences with biological and pharmaceutical interests. The association publishes *Science Magazine*.

AMERICAN SOCIETY FOR HORTICULTURAL SCIENCE

701 North St. Asaph Street

Alexandria, Virginia 22314

Telephone: (703) 836-4606

Description: Interests include breeding, growth and development, and genetics of crop plants.

AMERICAN SOCIETY OF AGRONOMY

677 South Segoe Road

Madison, Wisconsin 53711

Telephone: (608) 274-1212

Description: The society is a nonprofit educational and scientific organization with primary interests in studying how to utilize plant and soil sciences to produce high quality food and fiber crops.

AMERICAN SOCIETY OF SUGAR BEET TECHNOLOGISTS

P.O. Box1546

Ft Collins, Colorado 80522

Telephone: (303) 482-8250

Description: Areas of interest include the production, processing

and research related to the sugar beet industry.

B

BEN FRANKLIN PARTNERSHIP PROGRAM OF PENNSYLVANIA

Department of Commerce

463 Forum Building

Harrisburg, Pennsylvania 17120

Telephone: (717) 787-4147

Description: The program adapts scientific research to commercial

ventures through the cooperation of industry, universities and the

state.

C

CARNEGIE INSTITUTION

Department of Plant Biology

Governor's Avenue & Searsville Road

Stanford, California 94305

Telephone: (415) 325-1521

Description: This institution is operated in affiliation with

Stanford University. Research areas include photosynthesis, and

plant molecular biology

CENTER FOR ADVANCED RESEARCH IN BIOTECHNOLOGY

Montgomery County Office of Economic Development

101 Monroe Street

Rockville, Maryland 20850

Telephone: (301) 251-2345

Description: The center is affiliated with the state of Maryland, National Bureau of Standards, and Montgomery County, with its purpose to support business and industry in the form of biotechnology research and assistance.

CENTER FOR INNOVATIVE TECHNOLOGY

P.O. Box 15373

Herndon, Virginia 22070

Telephone: (703) 661-8994

Description: The purpose of this program is to bridge the gap between the transfer of science from university laboratories to applications in industry.

CLEMSON UNIVERSITY

South Carolina Agricultural Experiment Station

104 Barre Hall

Clemson, South Carolina 29631

Telephone: (803) 656-3140

Description: The agricultural experiment station does research in plant pathology and plant physiology.

COLORADO STATE UNIVERSITY

Department of Agronomy

Ft Collins, Colorado 80523

Telephone: (303) 491-6501

Description: This department does research on field crops, plant
genetics, crop physiology, and plant breeding.

CONGRESSIONAL BUDGET OFFICE

2nd and D Streets, S.W.

Washington, D.C. 20515

Telephone: (202) 226-2600

Description: This legislative office provides reports and budgetary
analysis in scientific areas of interest.

CONNECTICUT AGRICULTURAL EXPERIMENT STATION

123 Huntington Street

P.O. Box 1106

New Haven, Connecticut 06504

Telephone: (203) 789-7214

Description: Performs research in plant genetics, & biochemistry.

CORNELL UNIVERSITY

Boyce Thompson Institute For Plant Research Library

Tower Road

Ithaca, New York 14853

Telephone: (607) 257-2030

Description: Interested in botany and related subjects such as biochemistry, agriculture, disease tolerance of plants, and crop yields.

CORNELL UNIVERSITY

Cornell Biotechnology Program

Baker Laboratory

Ithaca, New York 14853

Telephone: (607) 256-2300

Description: This program has two components—one is sponsored by the state's Science and Technology Foundation and the other is supported by three industrial corporations to do research in the field of biotechnology.

CORNELL UNIVERSITY

International Agricultural Program

261 Roberts Hall

Ithaca, New York 14853

Telephone: (607) 256-2283

Description: Research activities include studies in the biological sciences. This program cooperates with foreign universities and colleges and has participated in student and staff exchanges.

CORNELL UNIVERSITY

New York State Agricultural Experiment Station

P.O. Box 462

Geneva, New York 14456

Telephone: (315) 787-2211

Description: This agricultural experiment station does research on plant pathology, and vegetable crops.

CORNELL UNIVERSITY

New York State Agricultural Experiment Station

292 Roberts Hall

Ithaca, New York 14853

Telephone: (607) 256 5420

Description: This agricultural experiment station does research in the biological sciences, plant pathology, biochemistry, and plant breeding.

E

ENVIRONMENTAL PROTECTION AGENCY

Office of Enforcement

401 M Street, S.W.

Washington, D.C. 20460

Telephone: (202) 382-2820

Description: This office deals with the enforcement of EPA's regulations and areas of responsibilities.

ENVIRONMENTAL PROTECTION AGENCY

Office of Pesticide Programs

401 M Street, S.W. (TS 766C)

Washington, D.C. 20460

Telephone: (202) 557-7090

Description: Responsible for programs to limit the use of pesticides if they affect the environment in an unhealthy way.

ENVIRONMENTAL PROTECTION AGENCY

Office of Research & Development

401 M Street, S.W.

Washington, D.C. 20460

Telephone: (202) 382-7676

Description: This office researches the effects of pollution in order to provide input to EPA on biotechnology regulatory issues.

ENVIRONMENTAL PROTECTION AGENCY

Office of Toxic Substances

401 M Street, S.W.

Washington, D.C. 20460

(202) 382-3813

Description: This office deals with development of the regulatory mechanism needed to handle genetic products as they effect the environment.

EXECUTIVE OFFICE OF THE PRESIDENT

Office of Management And Budget

Executive Office Building

Washington, D.C. 20503

Telephone: (202) 395-4840

Description: The purpose of OMB is to assist in the development and supervision of the President's budget, and in development of regulatory guidelines.

EXECUTIVE OFFICE OF THE PRESIDENT

Office Of Science Technology And Policy

Executive Office Building

Washington, D.C. 20500

Telephone: (202) 456-7116

Description: This office is involved in the issues of science and technology policy that pertain to the biotechnology field.

F

FLORIDA STATE UNIVERSITY

Institute of Molecular Biophysics

Tallahassee, Florida 32306

Telephone: (904) 644-4764

Description: Areas of interest include molecular biology, genetics, and photosynthesis.

G

GENERAL ACCOUNTING OFFICE

441 G Street N.W.

Washington, D.C. 20548

Telephone: (202) 275-2812

Description: This office overseas and reviews national issues of importance in science and technology.

H

HIGH PLAINS RESEARCH FOUNDATION

HC01-Box 117

Plainview, Texas 79072

Telephone: (806) 889-3316

Description: This Foundation answers inquiries on irrigation, plant genetics, and agricultural production.

HOUSE BUDGET COMMITTEE

House Annex #1

Washington, D.C. 20515

Telephone: (202) 226-7200

Description: The committee deals with budget issues and policies pertaining to science and technology.

HOUSE COMMITTEE ON AGRICULTURE

Longworth House Office Building

Washington, D.C. 20215

Telephone: (202) 225-2171

Description: This committee has jurisdiction over agriculture,

plants, seeds, and forestry.

HOUSE COMMITTEE ON APPROPRIATIONS

Capitol Building

Washington, D.C. 20515

Telephone: (202) 225-2771

Description: This committee deals with the appropriations of

Federal agencies involved in biotechnology.

HOUSE COMMITTEE ON SCIENCE AND TECHNOLOGY

2321 Rayburn House Office Building

Washington, D.C. 20515

Telephone: (202) 225-6371

Description: This committee has authority over the National

Bureau of Standards, NASA, NSF, and studies issues on research

and development.

I

INDIANA CORPORATION FOR SCIENCE AND TECHNOLOGY

1 North Capitol Avenue

Indianapolis, Indiana 46204

Telephone: (317) 635-3058

Description: The corporation is a private non-profit organization formed to support R&D ventures in the state of Indiana.

INDUSTRIAL BIOTECHNOLOGY ASSOCIATION

2115 East Jefferson Street

Rockville, Maryland 20852

Telephone: (202) 984-9599

Description: The association has members involved in biotechnology, and publishes materials and conducts workshops.

IOWA STATE UNIVERSITY OF SCIENCE AND TECHNOLOGY

Department of Agronomy

Ames, Iowa 50011

Telephone: (515) 294-1360

Description: Areas of interest include crop production, physiology, plant breeding, plant cytogenetics, and germplasm preservation.

IRI RESEARCH INSTITUTE

169 Greenwich Avenue

Stamford, Connecticut 06902

Telephone: (203) 327-5985

Description: The institute is a non-profit international research and development organization supported by the U.S., foreign governments, international banking organizations, and individuals. Involved in research activities that are directed to increasing crop production in developing countries.

K

KANSAS STATE UNIVERSITY

Agricultural Experiment Station

Waters Hall

Manhattan, Kansas 66506

Telephone: (913) 532-6191

Description: The agricultural experiment station studies wheat germplasm, cell cultures, and works on developing mutants and clones.

L

LABORATORY FOR INFORMATION SCIENCE IN AGRICULTURE

419 Canyon Road

Fort Collins, Colorado 80521

Telephone: (303) 224-9400

Description: The laboratory does crop research and genetics.

LIBRARY OF CONGRESS

Congressional Research Service

Washington, D.C. 20540

Telephone: (202) 287-7130

Description: CRS provides reports and research studies in the scientific and technical areas to Congress.

LIBRARY OF CONGRESS

National Referral Center

Washington, D.C. 20540

Telephone: (202) 287-5670

Description: The center maintains and provides information sources in all the scientific and technical fields.

M

MICHIGAN STATE UNIVERSITY

Biology Research Center

East Lansing, Michigan 48824

Telephone: (517) 355-2149

Description: The research center does research on plant genetics.

MICHIGAN STATE UNIVERSITY

Institute of International Agriculture

101 Agriculture Hall

East Lansing, Michigan 48824

Telephone: (517) 355-0174

Description: The institute supports research and instructional services in agricultural sciences and natural resources.

MICHIGAN STATE UNIVERSITY

Michigan Agricultural Experiment Station

East Lansing, Michigan 48824

Telephone: (517) 355-0123

Description: The agricultural experiment station does research on plant breeding, diseases, and production.

MICHIGAN STATE UNIVERSITY

Michigan Biotechnology Institute

276 Bessey Hall

East Lansing, Michigan 48824

Telephone: (517) 355-2277

Description: MBI coordinates the state of Michigan activities with Michigan State University, and does research on recombinant DNA.

MICHIGAN STATE UNIVERSITY

MSU-DOE Plant Research Laboratory

103 Plant Biology Building

East Lansing, Michigan 48824

Telephone: (517) 353-2270

Description: MSU works with the Department of Energy on basic plant research and studies the environmental effects on plants.

MONTANA STATE UNIVERSITY

College of Agriculture

Agriculture Experiment Station

Bozeman, Montana 59717

Telephone: (406) 994-3681

Description: Research is underway in plant breeding, plant pathology, and in the biological control of weeds.

N

NATIONAL ACADEMY OF SCIENCES

2100 Pennsylvania Ave. N.W.

Washington, D.C., 20550

Telephone: (202) 334-3318

Description: The Academy's Board on Agriculture and National Research Council advises the Federal government on scientific issues and keeps the public informed. The Academy published a book entitled *Genetic Engineering Of Plants*.

NATIONAL ASSOCIATION OF STATE UNIVERSITIES & LAND GRANT
COLLEGES

1 Dupont Circle N.W.

Washington, D.C. 20036

Telephone: (202) 293-7120

Description: The association has a division of agriculture with a
committee on biotechnology. The association published a report
entitled *Emerging Biotechnologies in Agriculture: Issues
and Policies (November 1984).*

NATIONAL COUNCIL OF COMMERCIAL PLANT BREEDERS

1030 15th Street N.W.

Washington, D.C. 20005

Telephone: (202) 223-4082

Description: The council promotes the interests of plant breeders
and provides information on research and development in progress
in this field.

NATIONAL FOREST PRODUCTS ASSOCIATION

1619 Massachusettes Avenue N.W.

Washington, D.C. 20036

Telephone: (202) 797-5800

Description: The association is concerned with national issues of
importance to the forest industry.

NATIONAL SCIENCE FOUNDATION

Directorate For Biological, Behavorial, and Social Sciences

1800 G Street N.W.

Washington, D.C. 20550

Telephone: (202) 357-9854

Description: NSF through this directorate supports research through grants in cellular biology, molecular biology, and biochemistry.

NATIONAL SCIENCE FOUNDATION

Directorate For Biological, Behavorial, and Social Science

Office of Biotechnology

1800 G Street N.W.

Washington, D.C. 20550

Telephone: (202) 357-9894

Description: This office serves as a focal point for a biotechnology information system and examines environmentally related basic research in biotechnology.

NATIONAL SCIENCE FOUNDATION

Directorate For Engineering

Office of Cross Disciplinary Research

1800 G Street N.W.

Washington, D.C. 20550

Telephone: (202) 357-9707

Description: This office is involved in programs that deal with targeted and non targeted biotechnology funding.

NATIONAL SCIENCE FOUNDATION

Directorate For Scientific and International Affairs

Division of International Programs

1800 G Street N.W.

Washington, D.C. 20550

Telephone: (202) 357-9700

Description: This section supports meetings and coordinates research efforts with foreign countries.

NATIONAL SCIENCE FOUNDATION

Industry/University Cooperative Research Projects Program

1800 G Street N.W.

Washington, D.C. 20550

Telephone: (202) 357-7784

Description: The objective of the program is to sponsor non-proprietary cooperative research projects between universities and industry.

NORTH CAROLINA BIOTECHNOLOGY CENTER

P.O. Box 13547

Research Triangle Park, North Carolina 27709

Telephone (919) 549-0671

Description: The staff maintains contact with public and private organizations conducting biotechnology related research.

O

OFFICE OF TECHNOLOGY AND ASSESSMENT

Biological Applications

600 Pennsylvania Ave S.E.

Washington, D.C. 20510

Telephone: (202) 226-2090

Description: The office studies the issues pertaining to genetic engineering and biotechnology, and has published a book entitled *Commercial Biotechnology An International Analysis.*

OHIO RESEARCH AND DEVELOPMENT CENTER

Ohio Department of Development

Thomas Alva Edison Partnership Program

P.O. Box 1001

Columbus, Ohio 43216

Telephone: (614) 466-3887

Description: The state is providing matching support for the formation of six centers through the R&D center.

OHIO STATE UNIVERSITY

Ohio Agriculture Research & Development Center

Wooster, Ohio 44691

Telephone: (216) 263-3701

Description: The center is presently working on a grant on the subject of genes and is doing research on plant breeding.

OREGON STATE UNIVERSITY

Department of Crop Science

Corvallis, Oregon 97331

Telephone: (503) 754-2821

Description: Interests in crop science, and plant genetics

P

PENNSYLVANIA STATE UNIVERSITY

Agricultural Research Center at Rock Springs

229 Agriculture Administration

University Park, Pennsylvania 16802

Telephone: (814) 865-5419

Description: The center has interests in plant pathology, breeding

and genetics.

PENNSYLVANIA STATE UNIVERSITY

Cooperative Program in rDNA Technology

616 Mueller Laboratory

University Park, Pennsylvania 16802

Telephone: (814) 865-1294

Description: The program is supported by industry and the

university and assists in technology transfer between the

university and industry research in rDNA and isolating genes that

specify disease resistance in plants.

S

SENATE APPROPRIATIONS COMMITTEE

S-128 Capitol Building

Washington, D.C. 20510

Telephone: (202) 224-3471

Description: The committee has authority over appropriations that deal with the agencies involved in agriculture.

SENATE BUDGET COMMITTEE

Dirkson Senate Office Building

SD 621

Washington, D.C. 20510

Telephone: (202) 224-0642

Description: The committee has authority over budget matters and legislative issues.

SENATE COMMITTEE ON AGRICULTURE, NUTRITION & FORESTRY

328-A Russell Senate Office Building

Washington, D.C. 20510

Telephone: (202) 224-2035

Description: The committee has authority over agriculture, agricultural products, pesticides, and forests.

SMALL BUSINESS ADMINISTRATION

Office of Investment

Small Business Investment Companies

1441 L Street N.W.

Washington, D.C. 20416

Telephone: (202) 653-6879

Description: The office makes venture capital available to small
companies involved in biotechnology.

SOUTH DAKOTA STATE UNIVERSITY

Department of Plant Sciences

Brooking, South Dakota 57006

Telephone: (605) 688-5121

Description: The department's interests are in field crop
production and management that include plant genetics, cytology,
cytogenetics, and plant pathology.

T

TEXAS A&M UNIVERSITY

Agricultural Research and Extension Center at Beaumont

Route 7, Box 999

Beaumont, Texas 77706

Telephone: (409) 752-2741

Description: The center studies rice genetics and breeding, and
soybean management.

TEXAS A&M UNIVERSITY

Beasley Laboratory

Department of Soil and Crop Science

College Station, Texas 77843

Telephone: (409) 845-2745

Description: The laboratory does research on cotton genetics.

TUSKEGEE INSTITUTE

Agricultural Experiment Station

206 Milbank Agriculture Hall

Tuskegee, Alabama 36088

Telephone: (205) 727-8334

Description: The agricultural experiment station is doing plant sciences research with emphasis on breeding genetics and nitrogen fixation.

U

U.S. DEPARTMENT OF AGRICULTURE

Agricultural Marketing Service

14th and Independence Avenue S.W.

Washington, D.C. 20250

Telephone: (202) 447-5115

Description: The service is involved in labeling seeds shipped by interstate and foreign commerce and grants patents for sexually reproduced varieties of plants.

U.S. DEPARTMENT OF AGRICULTURE

Agricultural Research Service

Arid Southwest Area, Alfalfa Research Center

University of Nevada

College of Agriculture

Reno, Nevada 89557

Telephone: (702) 784-5336

Description: Interests include alfalfa genetics, theory, autotetraploid genetics, and tissue cultures.

U.S DEPARTMENT OF AGRICULTURE

Agricultural Research Service

Arid Southwest Area, Cotton Research Center

4207 East Broadway

Phoenix, Arizona 85040

Telephone: (602) 261-4221

Description: Performs agricultural research on cotton plant pathology, plant physiology, weed control, and plant genetics.

U.S. DEPARTMENT OF AGRICULTURE

Agricultural Research Service

Beltsville Agricultural Research Center

Plant Genetics & Germplasm Institute

Beltsville, Maryland 20705

Telephone: (301) 344-3235

Description: The institute is responsible for collection, conservation and improvement of plants and seeds by genetic and cultural methods.

U.S. DEPARTMENT OF AGRICULTURE

Agricultural Research Service

Beltsville Agricultural Research Center

Plant Genetics and Germplasm Institute

Germplasm Resources Information Network (GRIN)

Beltsville, Maryland 20705

Telephone: (301) 344-3318

Description: GRIN is an electronic seed/plant catalog managed by ARS and contains information on the characteristics of over 600,000 plant samples collected worldwide.

U.S. DEPARTMENT OF AGRICULTURE

Agricultural Research Service

Beltsville Agricultural Research Center

Plant Genetics and Germplasm Institute

Germplasm Resources Laboratory

Beltsville, Maryland 20705

Telephone: (301) 344-4419

Description: The laboratory is a national contact point for information on plants and seeds.

U.S. DEPARTMENT OF AGRICULTURE

Agricultural Research Service

Beltsville Agricultural Research Center

Plant Physiology Institute

Beltsville, Maryland 20705

Telephone: (301) 344-3036

Description: The institute performs research on agricultural plants, plant physiology, plant genetics and genetic engineering.

U.S. DEPARTMENT OF AGRICULTURE

Agricultural Research Service

Imperial Valley Conservation Research Center

4151 Highway 86

Brawley, California 92227

Telephone: (714) 344-4184

Description: The center studies new and improved soil, water, and plant management practices for irrigated desert areas.

U.S. DEPARTMENT OF AGRICULTURE

Agricultural Research Service

National Seed Storage Laboratory

Colorado State University Campus

Fort Collins, Colorado 80523

Telephone: (303) 484-0402

Description: The center studies seed longevity, germplasm resources, seed storage equipment, seed germination requirements, and seed physiology, cryogenic storage, and genetic shifts.

U.S DEPARTMENT OF AGRICULTURE

Agricultural Research Service

Northeastern Regional Information Office

Beltsville Agricultural Research Center

Beltsville, Maryland 20705

Telephone: (301) 344-2264

Description: Areas of interest include research on livestock, crops, ornamental plants, pesticides and biological control of pests, soil, and water conservation research, and genetic engineering research.

U.S. DEPARTMENT OF AGRICULTURE

Agricultural Research Service

Tropical Agricultural Research Station

P.O. Box 70

Mayaguez, Puerto Rico 00708

Telephone: (809) 832-2435

Description: The station conducts research on plant breeding, agronomy, plant germplasm, and genetics.

U.S. DEPARTMENT OF AGRICULTURE

Agricultural Research Service

Western Regional Research Center

800 Buchanan Street

Albany, California 94710

Telephone: (415) 486-3856

Description: Performs basic and applied research on food, plants, and fibers. Project interests include plant growth hormones and regulators, nitrogen fixation, and photosynthesis

U.S. DEPARTMENT OF AGRICULTURE

Agricultural Research Service

Western Regional Research Center

Plant Gene Expression Center

Albany, California 94710

Telephone: (415) 486-3354

Description: The center is a joint venture with ARS, University of California and the California Agricultural Experiment Station, and will study the complex biology of plant expression.

U.S. DEPARTMENT OF AGRICULTURE

Animal & Plant Health Inspection Service

14th and Independence Avenue S.W.

Washington, D.C. 20250

Telephone: (202) 447-2511

Description: The service has the authority to control the spread of plant pests.

U.S. DEPARTMENT OF AGRICULTURE

ARS Patent Program

Building 003, Barc W

Beltsville, Maryland 20705

Telephone: (301) 344-2786

Description: This program has information available on government patents resulting from agricultural research, and provides a catalog of USDA inventions available for licensing.

U.S. DEPARTMENT OF AGRICULTURE

Cooperative State Research Service

Plant and Animal Sciences

14th and Independence Avenue S.W.

Washington, D.C. 20250

Telephone: (202) 447-4423

Description: CSRS administers research grant programs for the state agricultural experiment stations, forestry schools, land grant colleges, and assists with agricultural research programs within USDA.

U.S. DEPARTMENT OF AGRICULTURE

Current Research Information System (CRIS)

NAL Building

Beltsville, Maryland 20745

Telephone: (301) 344-3846

Description: CRIS is an agricultural data base with agricultural information that is sponsored by USDA research agencies, state organizations and other cooperating state institutions.

U.S. DEPARTMENT OF AGRICULTURE

Forest Service

Timber Management Research

Genetics and Related Research

14th and Independence Avenue S.W.

Washington, D.C. 20250

Telephone: (202) 235-8200

Description: This office does research on rDNA methodologies for transfer of genes in forest tree species.

U.S. DEPARTMENT OF AGRICULTURE

Joint Council on Food and Agricultural Sciences

14th and Independence Avenue S.W.

Washington, D.C. 20250

Telephone: (202) 447-5923

Description: The council coordinates research, and higher educational activities in the food and agricultural sciences. The council publishes reports that identify the needs for an effective food and agricultural system.

U.S. DEPARTMENT OF AGRICULTURE

National Agricultural Library

Information Systems Division

10301 Baltimore Blvd

Beltsville, Maryland 20705

Telephone: (301) 344-3355

Description: Topics covered in all subject areas of agriculture, forestry, plants, and agricultural chemistry and engineering.

U.S. DEPARTMENT OF AGRICULTURE

National Plant Genetic Resources Board

Beltsville Agricultural Research Center

Beltsville, Maryland 20705

Telephone: (301) 344-1560

Description: The board advises the Secretary of Agriculture and leaders of the National Association of State Universities and Land Grant Colleges on plant genetics.

U.S. DEPARTMENT OF AGRICULTURE

Office Of International Cooperation & Development (OICD)

14th and Independence Ave S.W.

Washington, D.C. 20250

Telephone: (202) 447-3157

Description: OICD conducts scientific exchange programs and administers a variety of international research programs.

U.S. DEPARTMENT OF AGRICULTURE

Recombinant DNA Advisory Committee

West Auditors Building

14th and Independence S.W.

Washington D.C. 20250

Telephone: (202) 447-5741

Description: This committee sets guidelines and polices of USDA applications and is involved in agricultural related biotechnology research.

U.S. DEPARTMENT OF AGRICULTURE

Science & Education Administration

14th and Independence Ave S.W.

Washington D.C. 20250

Telephone: (202) 447-5923

Description: Coordinates agricultural reseach as it relates to energy, economics, forestry plant production and aqaculture.

U.S. DEPARTMENT OF AGRICULTURE

Users Advisory Board

14th and Independence Avenue S.W.

Washington, D.C. 20250

Telephone: (202) 447-3684

Description: The board reviews policies, plans, and goals of research, and serves as consultants to the Secretary of Agriculture, and advises Congress.

U.S. DEPARTMENT OF COMMERCE

International Trade Administration

14th and Constitution Ave N.W.

Washington, D.C. 20230

Telephone: (202) 377-5087

Description: ITA has information available through a series of reports that describe agricultural activities in foreign countries.

U.S. DEPARTMENT OF COMMERCE

International Trade Administration

Export Enforcement

14th and Constitution Avenue N.W.

Washington, D.C. 20230

Telephone: (202) 377-3618

Description: The office assists with export licensing matters and answers questions on export regulations.

U.S. DEPARTMENT OF COMMERCE

National Bureau of Standards

Route 270 & Quince Orchard Road

Washington, D.C. 20234

Telephone: (301) 921-1000

Description: NBS develops standards for instrumentation that are used in the biotechnology field.

U.S. DEPARTMENT OF COMMERCE

National Technical Information Service

5285 Port Royal Road

Springfield, Virginia 22161

Telephone: (703) 487-4600

Description: NTIS provides information on U.S. government sponsored R&D reports from federal agencies in the areas of agriculture and other sciences.

U.S. DEPARTMENT OF COMMERCE

Patent and Trademark Office

Office of Technology Assessment and Forecast

Washington, D.C. 20231

Telephone: (703) 557-4414

Description: The office assembles, analyzes and makes available data concerning the patent file, and they published a patent profile on six areas of biotechnology involving enzymes and micro-organisms.

U.S. DEPARTMENT OF ENERGY

Assistant Secretary For Conservation & Renewable Energy

Office of Renewable Technology

Office of Biomass Energy Technology

1000 Independence Avenue S.W.

Washington, D.C. 20585

Telephone: (202) 252-6750

Description: The office does research and development on organic materials and how they can be converted into other products.

U.S. DEPARTMENT OF ENERGY

Assistant Secretary For Environment, Safety, and Policy

Office of Energy Research

Office of Basic Energy Sciences

Washington, D.C. 20545

Telephone: (301) 353-2873

Description: The office performs research and development in biological energy.

U.S. DEPARTMENT OF ENERGY

Assistant Secretary For Environment, Safety, and Policy

Office of Energy Research

Office of Health and Environmental Research

Washington, D.C. 20545

Telephone: (301) 353-3251

Description: Researches pollutants in the environment as they affect the population.

U.S DEPARTMENT OF HEALTH AND HUMAN SERVICES

Food And Drug Administration

Office of Regulatory Affairs

5600 Fishers Lane

Rockville, Maryland 20857

Telephone: (301) 443-3480

Description: The office is involved in monitoring and enforcing regulatory policies at FDA.

U.S. DEPARTMENT OF HEALTH AND HUMAN SERVICES

National Institutes Of Health (NIAID/ORDA)

Recombinant DNA Advisory Committee

9000 Rockville Pike

Bethesda, Maryland 20205

Telephone: (301) 496- 6051

Description: The committee advises on biological and environmental problems of dealing with rDNA and helps to devise guidelines for scientists involved in genetic engineering projects.

U.S. DEPARTMENT OF STATE

Bureau of International Organization Affairs

Agricultural Development Division

Office of International Development

2201 C Street N.W.

Washington, D.C. 20520

Telephone: (202) 632-0492

Description: The office deals with the United Nations agricultural organizations.

U.S. DEPARTMENT OF STATE

Bureau of Oceans & International Environmental & Scientific Affairs

Office of Science and Technology

2201 C Street N.W.

Washington, D.C. 20520

Telephone: (202) 632-2958

Description: The office deals with cooperative agreements with foreign countries in several areas of R & D.

UNIVERSITY OF CALIFORNIA (BERKELEY)

Agricultural Experiment Station

College of Natural Resources

Berkeley, California 94720

Telephone: (415) 642-7171

Description: The agricultural experiment station studies plant genetics, photosynthesis, cell biology, and molecular plant biology.

UNIVERSITY OF CALIFORNIA (DAVIS)

Agricultural Experiment Station

Davis, California 95616

Telephone: (916) 752-0107

Description: The agricultural experiment station does agricultural research in the plant and biological sciences.

UNIVERSITY OF CALIFORNIA (DAVIS)

Plant Growth Laboratory

Davis, California 95616

Telephone: (916) 752-6160

Description: The laboratory studies genetics in crop plants using DNA techniques to study bacteria and plants.

UNIVERSITY OF CALIFORNIA (RIVERSIDE)

Department of Botany and Plant Sciences

Riverside, California 92521

Telephone: (714) 787-4413

Description: Researchers study plant breeding and tissue cultures.

UNIVERSITY OF CONNECTICUT

Department of Plant Science

Storrs, Connecticut 06268

Telephone: (203) 486-2924

Description: The department is interested in genetics and plant breeding.

UNIVERSITY OF FLORIDA

Citrus Research & Education Center

700 Experiment Station Road

Lake Alfred, Florida 33850

Telephone: (813) 956-1151

Description: The center is studying plant physiology, pathology, and genetics.

UNIVERSITY OF FLORIDA

· Institute of Food and Agricultural Sciences

Route 4, Box 63

Monticello, Florida 32344

Telephone: (904) 997-2596

Description: The institute studies plant pathology, and breeding.

UNIVERSITY OF GEORGIA

Agricultural Experiment Station

College of Agriculture

Athens, Georgia 30602

Telephone: (404) 542-2151

Description: The agricultural experiment station is involved in general agriculture, agricultural engineering, agronomy, and plant pathology.

UNIVERSITY OF ILLINOIS

Department of Agronomy

Crop Evolution Laboratory

Urbana, Illinois

Telephone: (217) 333-4376

Description: The laboratory is involved in the genetics of cultivated plants and weeds.

UNIVERSITY OF KENTUCKY

College of Agriculture

Department of Agronomy

Lexington, Kentucky 40506

Telephone: (606) 258-9000

Description: The department is interested in agronomy, soil science, and plant genetics.

UNIVERSITY OF MARYLAND

Maryland Agricultural Experiment Station

College Park, Maryland 20742

Telephone (301) 454-3707

Description: The agricultural experiment station does research on plants and crops and is involved in genetic engineering.

UNIVERSITY OF MASSACHUSETTS

College of Food And Natural Resources

Department of Plant And Soil Sciences

Amherst, Massachusetts 01003

Telephone: (413) 545-2243

Description: The department is involved in plant breeding, plant physiology, plant nutrition, growth regulators, & soil sciences.

UNIVERSITY OF NEBRASKA

Nebraska Agricultural Experiment Station

High Plains Agriculture Laboratory

Route 1, Box 112A

Sidney, Nebraska 69162

Telephone: (308) 254-3918

Description: The laboratory is interested in agricultural research, agronomy, plant genetics, seeds, and grain crops.

UNIVERSITY OF NEVADA

College of Agriculture

Reno, Nevada 89557

Telephone: (702) 784-5336

Description: Areas of interest include alfalfa genetics, genetic theory, autotetraploid genetics, tissue cultures, seed production and plant breeding.

UNIVERSITY OF TEXAS (AUSTIN)

Genetics Institute

Austin, Texas 78712

Telephone: (512) 471-5420

Description: The institute does research and graduate training in biochemistry and molecular genetics.

UNIVERSITY OF WISCONSIN (MADISON)

Department of Plant Pathology

Plant Disease Resistance Research Center

Madison, Wisconsin 53706

Telephone: (608) 262-1541

Description: The department is studying diseases in plants and genetic engineering.

V

VIRGINIA POLYTECHNIC INSTITUTE AND STATE UNIVERSITY

Agricultural Experiment Station

Blacksburg, Virginia 24061

Telephone: (703) 961-6337

Description: The agricultural experiment station does research in plant pathology, biochemistry, microbiology, and genetics.

W

WASHINGTON STATE UNIVERSITY

College of Agriculture

Pullman, Washington 99164-6242

Telephone: (509) 335-4561

Description: The college of agriculture is involved in plant biotechnology research. The state legislature established the Washington Technology Center which plans to promote biotechnological research in crop plants and forest products. The funding level is expected to be $1 million dollars by the end of the 1980's and this total is expected to be matched from federal and industry sources bringing the total to $3 million dollars per year.

WORLD BIOLOGICAL SOCIETY

3615 Carson Drive

Amarillo, Texas 79109

Telephone: (806) 355-9369

Description: The society answers inquiries that pertain to research in genetic engineering.

Appendix B

ARS Area Administrative Offices

Beltsville Area Office
Room 209, Building 003
Beltsville, MD 20705
Telephone: (301) 344-3347

Central Plains Area Office
P.O. Box 70, RR #2
Dayton Road
Ames, IA 50010
Telephone: (515) 862-8558

Mid South Area Office
Stoneville Road
Stoneville, MS 38776
Telephone: (601) 497-2338

Midwest Area Office
1815 N. University Street
Peoria, IL 61604
Telephone: (309) 360-4208

Mountain States Area Office
2625 Redwing Road,
Ft. Collins, CO 80526
Telephone: (303) 323-5265

North Atlantic Area Office
600 East Mermaid Lane
Philadelphia, PA 19118
Telephone: (215) 489-6549

Northern States Area Office
15 South 5th Street
Minneapolis, MN 55402
Telephone: (612) 787-3600

Northwest Area Office
809 NE 6th Avenue
Portland, OR 97232
Telephone: (503) 429-2185

Pacific Basin Area Office
800 Buchanan Street
Albany, CA 94710
Telephone: (415) 449-3774

South Atlantic Area Office
P.O. Box 5677
Athens, GA 30613
Telephone: (404) 250-3322

Southern Plains Area Office
P.O. Box EC
College Station, TX 77841
Telephone: (409) 527-1343

Appendix C

State Agricultural Experiment Stations Under the Hatch Act of 1887

State agricultural experiment stations at these locations are the recipients of Hatch Act, Regional Research, and Research Facilities funds, and can participate in the Special and Competitive Grants Programs that is the responsibility of the Cooperative State Research Service. Note: New Haven Connecticut (SAES) is not affiliated with a land grant university.

University of Alaska
Fairbanks, Alaska 99701

American Samoa Community
  College
American Samoa, 96799

University of Arizona
Tucson Arizona 85721

Auburn University
Auburn, Alabama 36849

University of California
Berkeley, California 94720

Clemson University
Clemson, S.C. 29631

Colorado State University
Fort Collins, Colorado 80523

New Haven, Connecticut 06504

University of Connecticut
Storrs, Connecticut 06268

Cornell University
Geneva, New York 14456

Cornell University
Ithaca, New York 14853

University of Delaware
Newark, Delaware 19711

University of the District
of Columbia
Washington, D.C. 20008

University of Florida
Gainesville, Florida 32611

University of Georgia
Athens, Georgia 30602

University of Guam
Agana, Guam 96913

University of Hawaii
Honolulu, Hawaii 96822

University of Idaho
Moscow, Idaho 83843

University of Illinois
Urbana, Illinois 61801

Iowa State University of
Science & Technology
Ames, Iowa 50011

Kansas State University
Manhattan, Kansas 66506

Kentucky State University
Lexington, Kentucky 40506

Louisiana State University
Baton Rouge, Louisiana 70893

University of Maine
Orono, Maine 04469

University of Maryland
College Park, Maryland 20742

University of Massachusetts
Amherst, Massachusetts 01003

Michigan State University
East Lansing, Michigan 48824

College of Micronesia
Eastern Caroline Islands 96941

University of Minnesota
St. Paul, Minnesota 55108

Mississippi State University
Mississippi State, Miss. 39762

University of Missouri
Columbia, Missouri 65211

Montana State University
Bozeman, Montana 59715

University of Nebraska
Lincoln, Nebraska 68583

University of Nevada
Reno, Nevada 89557

University of New Hampshire
Durham, New Hampshire 03824

New Mexico State University
Las Cruces, New Mexico 88003

North Carolina State University
Raleigh, North Carolina 27650

North Dakota State University
Fargo, North Dakota 58105

Ohio Agricultural Research
 & Development Center
Wooster, Ohio 44691

Ohio State University
Columbus, Ohio 43210

Oklahoma State University
Stillwater, Oklahoma 74074

Oregon State University
Corvallis, Oregon 97331

Pennsylvania State University
University Park, Pa 16802

University of Puerto Rico
Rio Piedras, P.R 00708

Purdue University
Lafayette, Indiana 47907

University of Rhode Island
Kingston, Rhode Island 02881

Rutgers-State University
New Brunswick, New Jersey 08903

South Dakota State University
Brookings, S.D. 57006

University of Tennessee
Knoxville, Tennessee 37901

Texas A&M University
College Station, Texas 77843

Utah State University
Logan, Utah 84322

University of Vermont
Burlington, Vermont 05405

College of Virgin Islands
St Croix, V.I. 00850

Virginia Polytechnic Institute
 & State University
Blacksburg, Virginia 24061

Washington State University
Pullman, Washington 99164

West Virginia University
Morgantown, West Virginia 26506

University of Wisconsin
Madison, Wisconsin 53706

University of Wyoming
Laramie, Wyoming 82071

Appendix D

List of Companies Involved in Agricultural Activities

Advanced Genetics Research
220 Livington Street
Berkeley, Ca. 94606

Advanced Genetics Sciences
P.O. Box 654
Greenwich, Conn. 06838

A.E. Staley Manufacturing Co.
2200 Eldorado Street
Decatur, Illinois 62525

Agri Business Research
28 W Juniper
Gilbert, Arizonia 85234

Agrigenetics
3375 Mitchell Lane
Boulder, Colorado 80301

Agrobiotics
2751 Maryland Avenue
Baltimore, Md. 21218

Allied Chemical Corp.
P.O Box 4000R
Morristown, N.J. 07960

Amalgamated Sugar Co.
P.O. Box 1520
Ogden, Utah 84402

American Cyanamid Co.
1 Cyanamid Plaza
Wayne, N.J. 07470

Amgen
1892 Oak Terrace La.
Newbury Park, Ca. 91320

Amstar Corporation
1251 Ave. of the Americas
New York, New York 10020

Applied Molecular Genetics
1900 Oak Terrace La.
Thousand Oaks, Ca. 9132

Archer Daniels Midland
4666 Faries Parkway
Decatur, Illinois 62525

ARCO Plant Cell Research Institute
 6560 Trinity Court
Dublin, Ca. 94568

Arco Solar Industries
911 Wilshire Blvd.
Los Angeles, Ca. 90051

Ashland Oil
P.O. Box 391
Ashland, Kentucky 41101

ATP-Syntro
11095 Torreyana Rd.
San Diego, Ca. 92121

Austin Company
3650 Mayfield
Cleveland, Ohio 44121

Barberton Technical Center
P.O. Box 31
Barberton, Ohio 44203

Battelle Memorial Institute
505 King Avenue
Columbus, Ohio 43201

Bioassay Systems Corp.
225 Wildwood Ave.
Woburn, Mass. 01801

Bio Con
3601 Gibson Street
Bakersfield, Ca. 93308

Bioferm International
P.O. Box 458
Medford, N.J. 08055

Biogen
241 Binney Street
Cambridge, Mass. 02142

Bio Systems Research
P.O. Drawer 1037
Salida, Colorado 81201

Biotechnica International
85 Boulton Street
Cambridge, Mass. 02140

Biotechnical Resources
7th & Marshall St.
Manitowac, Wisc. 54220

Biotechnology General Corp.
280 Park Avenue
New York, New York 10017

Calgene
1910 Fifth St.
Davis, Ca. 95616

Cambridge Bioscience
225 Longwood Avenue
Boston, Mass 02140

Campbell Soup Co.
Campbell Rd.
Camden, N.J. 08101

Centaur Genetics Corp.
120 S. LaSalle St.
Chicago, Illinois 60603

Cetus Madison
2208 Parkview Rd.
Middleton, Wisc. 53562

Cheron Corporation
4560 Horton Street
Emeryville, Ca. 94608

Ciba Geigy
444 Saw Mill River Rd.
Ardsley, New York 10502

Clinton Corn Processing
600 31st Street
Chicago, Illinois 60602

Collaborative Research
128 Spring Street
Lexington, Mass. 02173

Continental Grain Co.
10 South Riverside Plaza
Chicago, Illinois 60606

Crop Genetics International
7170 Standard Drive
Dorsay, Maryland 21076

Dairyland Food Laboratories
620 Progress Avenue
Waukeska, Wisc. 53187

Davy McKee Corporation
6200 Oak Tree Blvd.
Cleveland, Ohio 44131

Dekalb Pfizer Genetics
Sycamore Rd.
Dekalb, Illinois 60115

Diamond Laboratories
2538 E. 43rd Street
Des Moines, Iowa 50314

Diamond Mills
P.O. Box 4408
Cedar Rapids, Iowa 52407

Dow Chemical Co.
2030 Dow Center
Midland, Michigan 48640

DNA Plant Technology
2611 Branch Pike
Cinnaminson, N.J. 08077

Ean-Tech
699-A Cerramonte Blvd
Dale City, Ca. 94015

Ecogen
1101 State Rd. Bldg. O
Princeton N.J. 08540

E.I. du Pont de Nemours
1007 Market Street
Wilmington, Del. 19898

Eli Lilly Company
307 East McCarty Street
Indianapolis, Indiana 46285

Enbio
230 Park Lane
Atherton, Ca. 94025

Engenics
2 Palo Alto Square
Palo Alto, Ca. 94304

Enzo Biochem
325 Hudson Street
New York, New York 10013

Enzyme Technology
11842 W. 85th Street
Overland, Kansas 66215

Fairchild Industries
20301 Century Blvd.
Germantown, Md. 20874

Fermentec Corporation
301 Saratoga Avenue
Los Gatos, California 95030

First Mississippi Corp.
700 North Street
Jackson, Miss. 39205

Fleischmann Yeast
625 Madison Avenue
New York, New York 10022

FMC Corporation
200 East Randolph Drive
Chicago, Illinois 60601

Frito Lay Inc.
P.O. Box 35034
Dallas, Texas 75235

Frost Technology
537 Newtown Avenue
Norwalk, Conn. 06852

Genencor
Baron Steuben Place
Corning, New York 14831

Genentech Inc.
460 Point San Bruno Blvd.
San Francisco, Ca. 94080

General Foods Corp.
250 North Street
White Plains, N.Y. 10625

Genetics Institutes
225 Longwood Avenue
Brookline, Mass. 02115

Genex Corporation
6110 Executive Blvd.
Rockville, Md. 20852

George J. Ball
P.O. Box 335
West Chicago, Illinois 60185

Grain Processing Corp.
1600 Oregon Street
Muscatine, Iowa 52761

Great Lakes Biochemical
P.O. Box 2200
West Lafayette, Indiana

Hoffman La Roche
340 Kinsland Street
Nutley, N.J. 07110

Hybritech Inc.
11085 Torreyana Rd
San Diego, Ca. 92121

Indiana BioLab
P.O. Box 407
Palmyra, Indiana 47164

Int'l Genetic Engineering
1701 Colorado Avenue
Santa Monica, Ca. 90404

Int'l Genetic Sciences Partnership
15525 Styler Rd.
Jamaica, New York 11433

International Minerals & Chemicals
2315 Sanders Rd.
Northbrook, Illinois 60062

Int'l Plant Research Institute
853 Industrial Rd.
San Carlos, Ca. 94070

Int'l Resource Development
30 High Street
Norwalk, Conn. 06852

ITT Rayonier
1177 Summer Street
Stamford, Conn. 06904

JoJoba Horizons
2990 E. Northern Avenue
Phoenix, Arizona 85028

Kellogg Corporation
235 Porter Street
Battle Creek, Michigan 49016

Koppers Company
436 7th Avenue
Pittsburgh, Pa. 15212

Kraft Company
Kraft Court
Glenview, Illinois 60025

Life Sciences
2900 72nd Street N
St.Petersburg, Fla. 33710

Liposome Technology Inc.
1030 Curtis Street
Menlo Park, California 94025

Lubrizol Enterprises
29400 Lakeland Blvd.
Wickliffe, Ohio 44094

Martin Marietta
680 Rockledge Drive
Bethesda, Md. 20034

McCormick Spice
11350 McCormick Rd
Hunt Valley, Md. 21031

Molecular Genetics
10320 Bren Rd East
Minnetonka, Minn. 55343

Monsanto Company
800 N. Linbergh
St. Louis, Mo. 63167

Multivac Inc.
P.O. Box 575
Seal Beach, Ca. 90740

Nabisco Inc.
River Rd and De Forest Ave.
East Hanover, N.J. 07936

Nat'l Distillers & Chemical Corp.
99 Park Avenue
New York, New York 10016

Neogen Corporation
1407 S. Harrison Rd.
East Lansing, Michigan 48824

NIE Plant Tissue Culture Lab
529 E 3rd Avenue
San Mateo, Ca. 94401

Novo Laboratories
59 Danbury Rd
Wilton, Conn. 06897

NPI
360 Wahara Way
Salt Lake City, Utah 84108

Nutri Search
1014 Vine Street
Cincinnati, Ohio 45201

Occidental Petroleum
10889 Wilshire Blvd
Los Angeles, Ca. 90024

Ocean Genetics
1990 N. California Blvd
Walnut Creek, Ca. 94596

Pennwalt Corporation
3 Parkway
Philadelphia, Pa. 19102

Phillips Petroleum Co.
Research Center
Bartlesville, Ok. 74004

Phytogen
101 Waverly Drive
Pasadena, Ca. 91105

Phyto-tech Lab
21822 South Vermont Ave.
Torrance, Ca. 90502

Pioneer Hi-Bred Int'l Inc.
700 Capital Square
400 Locust Street
Des Moines, Iowa 50309

Plant Genetics
1930 5th Street
Davis, Ca. 95616

Ralston Purina
Checkerboard Square
835 S 8th Street
St. Louis, Missouri 63188

R&A Plant/Soils
Box 1001
Pasco, Wa. 99301

Repligen Corp
101 Binney Street
Cambridge, Mass. 02142

R.J. Reynolds Industry
Reynolds Blvd.
Winston Salem, N.C. 27102

Rohm & Haas
Independence Mall
W. Philadelphia, Pa. 19105

Salk Institute Biotechnology/
   Industrial Associates Inc.
P.O. Box 85200
San Diego, Ca. 92037

Sandoz Inc.
Route No. 10
East Hanover, N.J. 07936

Sigco Research
Box 289
Breckenridge, Minnesota 56520

Stauffer Chemical Company
Nyala Farms Road
Westport, Conn. 06880

Sugene Technologies Corp.
3330 Hillview Avenue
Palo Alto, Ca. 94304

Synergen
1885 Thirty Third Street
Boulder, Colorado 80301

Syngene Products & Research
225 Commerce Drive
Fort Collins, Colorado 80522

U.S. Agri Research
1 Newport Place
Newport Beach, Ca. 92660

Universal Foods
433 E Michigan Street
Milwaukee, Wisc. 53202

University Genetics Co.
537 Newtown Avenue
Norwalk, Conn. 06852

Vulcan Cincinnati
2900 Vernon Place
Cincinnati, Ohio 45219

Weyerhauser Company
2525 A 336th Street
Tacoma, Washington 98477

Worne Biotechnology Inc.
P.O. Box 458
Medford, N.J. 08055

W.R. Grace & Company
7379 Route 32
Columbia, Md. 21044

Xenogen Inc.
557 Wormwood Rd.
Mansfield, Conn. 08055

Zoecon Corp.
975 California Avenue
Palo Alto, Ca. 94304

Index